JOY IS MY ANSWER

....

WHAT I LEARNED FROM THE REFINER'S FIRE

A SPIRITUAL MEMOIR

LAURA STOKER

JIMA Books
PAYSON, UTAH

Grateful acknowledgment is made for permission to reproduce the cover of the March/April 2014 issue of *Networking Times*.

Laura Stoker/JIMA Books
www.laurastoker.com
laura@laurastoker.com

Cover design by Gus Yoo
Cover photo by Casey Robertson
Copy editing and production by Stephanie Gunning
Book Layout © Book Design Templates

Ordering Information: Special discounts are available on quantity purchases by corporations, associations, and others.

ISBN 978-0-578-54831-9
Library of Congress Control Number 2019910554
Joy Is My Answer/Laura Stoker. —1st ed.

To God

*To Brianna, Caitlyn, Alyssa, Emma,
Grace, and Wesley*

"Remember, O Lord, thy tender mercies and thy lovingkindnesses; for they have been ever of old."
–PSALM 25:6, OLD TESTAMENT

"Tender mercies of the Lord are over all those whom he hath chosen, because of their faith, to make them mighty even unto the power of deliverance."
–1 NEPHI 1:20, BOOK OF MORMON

CONTENTS

AUTHOR'S NOTE

Some of the names and identifying characteristics of people mentioned in this book have been changed to protect their privacy. The stories are true.

Periodically, you will see me refer to the *veil*. By this term, I mean our perception of separation between our earthly existence and our spiritual home, which some call *heaven*.

ACKNOWLEDGMENTS

This book wouldn't be possible without the contributions of many people.

First, I would like to express my deep appreciation to my family and my extended family, who lived the story with me. To my deceased husband, Wade, who was the father of my children, thank you for the lessons—the joy, the sorrow, and even the pain. If not for our journey together, I would not be the woman I am today. I am also grateful to each of my children, who remind me of my mission in life every day. I love you to the moon and back, Brianna, Caitlyn, Alyssa, Emma, Grace, and Wesley. To my sweet grandson, Silas. I love you. Thank you, Mom and Dad, for always holding me up, teaching me, and loving me unconditionally. I am also so grateful for my wonderful husband Matt, who loves me completely, has embraced my broken heart and all my quirks, crazy ideas, and passion! You were indeed divinely prepared for me and for my children. I adore every part of you! And to my bonus daughters, Lindsey,

Whitney, and Elle, I am so grateful that when I married your dad you joined my family too.

My dear friend Rachelle Castor, you are my angel on this side of the veil! Thank you for reminding me that I want light and that I am never alone.

I am grateful to my dear friends (specifically Spring and Amy) who walked a similar road before me and were there to help hold me up and offer encouragement in my darkest hours.

Many thanks to my amazing editor, Stephanie Gunning!

Much appreciation to my dōTERRA family! I am humbled and grateful to be part of dōTERRA!

Thank you to my Peru friends.

Finally, to my Father in heaven and to my heavenly brother, Jesus Christ. I know, like I have never known before, that you are real, that you live, and that your love is available to everyone! Thank you for quite literally carrying me during my darkest hours. Thank you for healing my heart. Thank you for providing angels to me just as I needed them—both on this side of the veil and the other side. Thank you for giving me the spiritual gifts to be able to feel and hear the whisperings of my guardian angels.

FOREWORD

It has been three years since my first husband, Wade, passed, and as I write, I am reliving the loss as if it happened yesterday. This experience thrust me into the refiner's fire. I certainly wouldn't have chosen my trials, and yet, in looking back over events, I can see why I was given them. Everything came from my Father in heaven. I have walked the road of grief and healing and been tremendously blessed in the process. With each choice I had to consider, an answer was provided to me. A beautiful part of it all has been opening to receive *spiritual downloads.*

I was speaking with a friend who explained the near-death experience of her own husband as being like this: Imagine you are at the most amazing and lively family reunion. You excuse yourself to use the bathroom. After a few minutes, you are done and rejoin your family. This "bathroom break" is your earthly life. The "family reunion" is your life in heaven. It is a joyful event. The human lifespan is like a few moments in the grand view of eternity! We exist long before we are born on earth and live on in eternity forever with our loved ones after we pass. Although it may seem that this life is all we have and all that is, that is *not* the case.

As you read my story in this book, please know that I have confidence now that comes from knowing I have God to lean on always, in every circumstance! I know I am part of a much bigger plan. I am here for a good reason. I am not alone in this life. My view has expanded. My paradigm has changed. I understand I am always worthy of God's love and companionship.

I was brought to my knees by a broken heart. I needed God, and he was there. He carried me unconditionally and without judgment as we know it in this life. My fear of losing a loved one was realized. Afterward, my eyes were opened. Now I know that the things of this world are insignificant in the bigger picture. To bury loved ones and to wipe away tears from my eyes and those of my children has given me more compassion than I could have ever imagined.

Without this experience, I also would not know the joy that I do now. How is it possible to experience so much joy in earthly life when there has also been so much tragedy and pain? What is joy? For me, joy is an internal daily choice that's not dependent on external events or other people. Joy does not come from having a charmed life without trials. It doesn't come from marrying the "perfect" man or having your children always choose to "do the right thing."

As a mother, the love that I feel for my children is unconditional despite my very human frailties. How much greater must God's eternal love be for us in his completely perfected state? When my children make choices that I know will cause them pain, do I turn my back to them when they reach out? No! I am always there, offering them my love and guidance. How is it that my belief most of my life was that I needed to earn my way to being worthy of God's love?

With humility, I can now say that I know that God loves me. Because he created me and knows me. And his son, Jesus Christ, is my biggest cheerleader. Literally, he is my advocate to my Father in heaven. He deeply loves me and accepts me just as I am. There is no "earning" my way to being worthy of His love. The moment I ask, he is there. I am unconditionally loved.

And so are you. You were created in the image of God. You are loved.

We are all spiritual beings having a human experience. Our physical bodies are finite. Meaning, there is a beginning and an end to them. We are born, we grow up, we age, we get sick, and eventually, we leave our mortal existence. However, that which we are continues on. We are infinite beings—meaning, there is no death. If at times you feel that you are being tested, let the refiner's fire purify you. Turn to heaven. Receive its gifts. Remember, you are worthy.

Laura Stoker
Payson, Utah
August 2019

ONE

....

AS A CHILD

It has been said that the two things people fear most are public speaking and death.

When I was in the first grade, a fellow classmate wasn't at school for what seemed like weeks. Our teacher announced that this young boy's brother had passed away unexpectedly. My heart ached for him. I felt so powerless. I wondered what had happened. The idea of this death haunted me, as it led me to imagine losing one of my siblings.

Raised in a Christian home, at an early age I was taught about the presence of a loving heavenly Father and that Jesus Christ was my Savior. My heavenly brother, he had sacrificed his life for me in the act of atonement. If I lived righteously, I could return home to our heavenly Father. Even so, I felt a sense of impending doom when I thought of dying myself that was suffocating. Death was my worst fear.

Much of my youth was spent playing outdoors with my siblings (four sisters and two brothers), cousins, and friends. We didn't have a television set until I was fourteen. My parents believed that we should work and play and not waste time sitting in front of a TV. I have a wonderful and close extended family on both sides of my family. Although all my grandparents have passed away, many decades later now, I still remain close to many of my cousins.

In the summers, working hard consisted of weeding a very large garden, during which toil we kids enjoyed many strawberry-throwing contests; taking care of the animals (we had goats, pigs, dogs, and many cats); and regular indoor chores, like making beds, washing dishes, folding laundry, and so on. Our days were filled with riding our bikes all over the community until sunset, camping, jumping in massive leaf piles, and attending exciting family reunions with my best friends who were also my cousins. I remember making forts, playing kick the can and tetherball, ziplining, riding four-wheelers, and being taken swimming at the local pool as a reward for a job well done. In winter, we'd go sledding.

My parents were industrious. In addition to being an avid genealogist, my mom baked countless loaves of bread that she sold to earn enough money to buy an upright piano. My dad ran a large family business with his dad and brother. He also was very involved in politics. He had a knack for woodworking and made things for us kids, including beds and baby cradles, and a board on which hung a list of our rotating chores. I earned an allowance by doing chores, which taught me the value of a dollar.

We lived in an old farmhouse which Mom and Dad had completely renovated. It sat on many acres of land. The driveway was unpaved and very long. Many of my most fun memories are of riding a zipline my dad had put up between some trees, which ran the length of the driveway. In the summertime, we would fill large canning jars that had little holes carefully punch in their lids with lightning bugs that we caught at dusk. We also would catch large frogs as we stomped around the fields.

In other words, I had a wonderful childhood growing up in Illinois. Sure, I had the typical insecurities a young girl sometimes has; I was shy and didn't feel like I was part of the popular crowd. I wasn't into trends or fashion and was perfectly content to wear a pair of blue jeans and a tee-shirt. I loved to read and struggled with math. For as long as I can remember, I held the belief that life was an adventure, and it would just get better and better as I got older. I was a dreamer and a country girl at heart.

Our move to Utah at the start of eighth grade was a culture shock for me. Attending my junior high in Springville, Utah, where everyone was predominately Mormon like we were, was surreal. My parents are wonderful people. They wanted us to be surrounded by other kids who shared similar religious beliefs and family values as ours. It was an exciting time, opening a completely new chapter in my life. I quickly acclimated. Our family rented a house while our dream home was built. My parents were very hands-on with the construction. They dreamed that this house would be ours forever, lasting through all their kids growing up and possibly even the raising of the grandchildren. We were to live on Osmond Lane in Provo.

Yes, the famous Osmonds were actually going to be our neighbors!

My dad continued to commute every week to Illinois for his job. As an adult, I now understand what a great sacrifice he made. The commutes took a toll on my parents' marriage, and soon, I found myself with parents who were heading for divorce. I felt as if the foundation of my world had been knocked out from under my feet. It was so painful that I swore then and there that I myself would never get divorced. I would marry a wonderful man who would be a perfect partner and start a family with him. I would never be "selfish" and get divorced. No matter what, I would stay with my husband forever and provide stability for my children. That's what I would tell myself.

Mom and Dad never stopped loving each other. After their divorce and twenty-four years of living apart, they remarried. The wedding was a beautiful ceremony in which all their kids and our spouses shed many happy tears. I recognize that this kind of recommitment is unusual, but I am so glad it happened for them. This event confirmed that when two people join their lives, share children and history, the connection runs very deep.

I always imagined that if I was ever to get divorced, I would have deep regrets.

TWO

....

OUR MARRIAGE

I met my husband Wade at twenty-two. I was working for my father's company as a secretary. Pete, the janitor, set us up. He was a kindly older man who had come to know Wade while Wade was serving a mission for the church in Provo, Utah. Our first meeting was on a blind date. Wade was tall, dark, and handsome. He was smart, too. He told me he wanted to be a doctor. He was the type of man I had dreamed of marrying as a little girl.

Our courtship was fast. We were engaged two months after meeting and got married two months after that on a cool, rainy day in spring 1994. In a matter of weeks, I got pregnant. It should have been a joyous period of my life, but something was not quite right. I couldn't quite put my finger on what was wrong. But within the first year, I felt uneasy about Wade's behavior. For one thing, he seemed disengaged. I wasn't happy with the amount of time he liked to be in front of the TV. But because he was smart, tall, dark, and handsome, I was sure things would get better.

Maybe my feeling of something being not quite right was my issue? I was always second-guessing myself. The birth of our first daughter, Brianna, was an adjustment. She was a healthy, beautiful nine-pound baby who had colic and cried continuously for what felt like several months. I really could have used more support from my husband.

Certain memories stand out to me. They will be etched into my mind forever. When Brianna was just a few months old, Wade explained to me that he was severely depressed. He said that he had never felt as low as he did at that moment. He was working part time at our local grocery store in the meat department. He expressed to me many times that his life was not what he had wanted and that he was "behind." He was resentful toward me because of it. That resentment would last for several years.

During our first years of marriage, he withdrew intimacy frequently. The absence of affection and communication was so severe that I spoke with our bishop about it, after which the bishop called Wade into his office and encouraged him to "love" me. There was a disconnect between us whose source was difficult to pinpoint. There were instances when things happened that I could not rationally explain. I was confused that things "felt" different than what I had imagined married life to be. But somehow, this state of affairs became our new normal. We gradually adjusted to a life of parenting together and vowed, "A divorce is never an option." Together we would make our marriage work. We agreed that people who got divorced were "being selfish."

This solidified my role in the marriage as the "pleaser." I was so determined to give my kids what I didn't have growing up—a family that stayed together— that I avoided conflict at my own expense.

Over the years, Wade and I welcomed four more daughters and a son. Wade truly loved being a father and a husband. Many memories were created in our household. One of the things we loved to do was get into a TV series on Netflix and watch it as a family. We would gather around and share popcorn.

Wade was an avid book reader. In particular, he loved science fiction. He shared a love with our older kids of attending the yearly Comic Con in our area. Frequently, he entertained us with his nunchuck skills. In fact, one Halloween, he performed on stage in our church talent show to one of his favorite rock songs. Wade's sense of humor and quick-witted nature had us laughing on those good days!

Wade encouraged each of our children to develop their individual talents. He had the crazy idea of purchasing Caitlyn a horse, even at the time we didn't have horse property. Another time, when she worked at a sales kiosk in the local shopping mall, he decided we would go visit her and purchase multiple items she was getting paid commission for (even though we didn't need the products). He was very concerned about each of our children and he truly had a kind heart.

When one child felt down and was having a bad day, he would leave a little note that almost always was silly and exactly what was needed for that child.

In his healthy state, he would make things happen.

A big part of our commitment to making our marriage work were weekly "hot dates," as Wade liked to call them. Even when money was tight, he found the resources to treat me to massages and delicious dinners at our favorite restaurants. He was there for every doctor's appointment during my pregnancies and the delivery of each of our six children.

On the one hand, it seemed that he would always be there—like I could count on him. On the other hand, he would isolate himself for hours at a time. He struggled to behave consistently.

I went into therapy. During a session with my therapist, he shared: "Trust is essential to have a successful relationship. Trust is when you can predict a person's behavior." Often, I was not able to predict Wade's behavior. He was on a roller-coaster ride of depressive episodes that sometimes included talk of suicide. Since I'd assumed the role of a people-pleaser, I was always looking for ways to help him because I thought I could save him and somehow it would get better. From day to day, his moods were different. Sometimes weeks would pass without him having an episode, but the isolation was always there.

Living with a man suffering from depression played tricks on my mind. I found myself having internal fantasies of a different life. I guilted myself over this and thought something surely must be wrong with me. My therapist said, "This is your mind's way of coping with your situation, and it is perfectly normal." I was not honest with myself. I shelved my own needs in favor of my husband's. Above all else, I was committed to doing whatever I needed to do to keep our marriage together. My mind had been programmed for this goal because I felt so sad as a child when my parents divorced. Come hell or high water, I stubbornly refused to change my commitment even to save myself and my kids from sinking with Wade's ship. I felt I had to do all that I could to protect my children from the pain of a broken family that I'd felt as a kid.

Every time Wade changed schools the family moved. With each move, we also started attending a new church, where I would eventually pour my heart out to the bishop and ask for advice. I desperately wanted to do what was right even if it meant my own sacrifice. One bishop shared something with me that I will always remember. As I sat across from him, tears flowing, expressing how mad I was at Wade, he counseled me: "Don't stay in your marriage for the sake of the kids."

"WOW! Really?" I asked.

He replied, "It never works."

I left feeling validated. I had been heard, and he could see it clearly that it wasn't a good thing for me to stay married to Wade. However, I still couldn't do it. I still could not justify leaving him and "breaking up the family."

The bishops in every church we attended were listening ears for me. Both Wade and I saw many different therapists. With every move so that he could attend a new school and with every other life change, I thought he would get better. I hoped he wouldn't withdraw as much and that he would be more involved.

If we had more money,

If we didn't have so much stress with the kids,

If his health was better,

If he lost weight,

Then he would be happy!

But the patterns never changed. That was what I could count on. The mood swings, the withdrawal of his affection and of his participation in the household.

A few times, we separated. He moved out of the house and stayed with a friend. Sometimes the separation would last for a week or two, sometimes for a few months. Then I would take him back. The longest separation was five months.

Each time we separated, Wade would begin to eat healthier and lose weight. His mood would improve, and when he came around, he would be wearing new clothes, cologne, and a smile, and he looked handsome. He would somehow become the man I had wanted to marry. I would see him make these changes. He also would commit to me that he would never again play video games or be unproductive. So, each time, my defenses were worn down. My boundaries would crumble, and I'd believe him when he promised me that things would be different.

And I would take him back.

This became such a pattern that my kids recognized it in the later years of the marriage. It would take my increasing awareness of exactly how our relationship was affecting them for my eyes to completely open to how destructive it was.

Further exacerbating the situation was a minor stroke that Wade suffered in 2008. After that, his physical health began to deteriorate, which was an additional source of stress for Wade.

At the time we conceived our son, our youngest child, Wade and I had been separated for several months, and I was moving forward with a divorce. We had five beautiful daughters and nineteen years of history, but I couldn't do it anymore. I finally decided to end my marriage. The mood swings had me walking on eggshells continually, and I couldn't keep it up anymore.

I explored the prospect of divorce with my therapist. The thought was unappealing. The idea gave me more anxiety than the idea of continuing to try to make my marriage work. But I was miserable. I didn't know what to do because I wanted to do the "right" thing. My therapist explained that the anxiety was to be expected. Moving forward with a divorce was like willingly going into battle. Of course, it seemed easier to stay with what was familiar.

While I was struggling with my decision, my defenses wore down. Wade swore to me that he wanted to work on our marriage. I gave him another chance. Our son was conceived after Wade came home in a period when I had complete faith and hoped we'd make the marriage work.

I was so confused and lost, and yet, from the outside, things seemed good. I was in denial. It was much easier to sweep things under the carpet. I believed my lie and then, to make it true, I became a people-pleaser. Some have called this the *disease to please*.

There were times when he would get really frustrated and angry and seem to explode. He never was physically abusive, but it felt very scary because he wasn't predictable. In those moments, when he was displaying his inability to manage his mood swings, I would freeze.

I remember breastfeeding one of my babies and hearing him explode at one of the older girls. He literally chased her up the stairs.

On that occasion, Wade had been playing video games in the basement for many hours. The kids were playing in the same room when he asked them to be quiet and clean up. They moved a little too slow in cleaning, and because he was gaming, his emotions got the best of him. I heard screaming and running up the stairs, but I couldn't get up because an infant was in my lap. I also didn't have courage or strength at that moment.

My normal pattern was to tell him to calm down, but I didn't follow through on holding him accountable for his behavior. I was afraid to confront the real issue, which was that he had a severe mental illness, and I was his enabler.

I played a part in Wade's dysfunction. I allowed it because I wanted to protect my children from the pain of divorce.

I thought I was being strong. I sacrificed my needs and happiness for the family. I imagined I was being noble and great, but I was in constant conflict because I was filled with anger. I would mutter under my breath what a "jerk" Wade was. If only *he* would change then things would be good! If only *he* would stop video game playing and be more involved. If only *he* would treat me better and be consistent so I could count on him!

My anger was directly toward what *he* should do. My finger was pointing at him. I didn't see what I was doing! I was the "victim" After all. He was just a big fat jerk! I was the noble one trying to continue work to "save" my family.

I tried to save him, too. I saw Wade as a hurt child that I couldn't simply kick to the curb. In my mind, I blamed him most of the time for our struggles. I even felt remorse and guilt when our daughter at age three was diagnosed with type 1 diabetes. I wondered if it came from his side of the family, then I later learned this was not the case!

I was trying to do everything "right." I believed that idealistic belief that if you did XYZ, then XYZ would happen. Things would be as they "should be" because you were righteous and noble.

I was intertwined in Wade's mental illness. I was relieved when he was up. When he went down and cycled, I became the pleaser. I walked on eggshells.

There were times that my anxiety got so high! I longed to be "normal."

Mental illness is so hard to put a finger on. On the outside it would seem things were fine. I wanted out, but I didn't feel justified in leaving. And I did love him, so I was torn up inside. It always came down to what he needed to do to "change."

There were conversations when I would ask Wade, "When do I get to be tired or weak?" Not that I wanted to be, but I wanted to feel safe and taken care of occasionally! Between severe depression, neck and back pain, anxiety, lack of energy and self-destructive behavior, he always had something to focus on and that thing was very rarely me.

And yet, I recognized I was doing this to myself. I was playing a key role in our unhealthy, codependent relationship. To this day, it is my biggest regret that I was a classic enabler.

I see the very damaging effect it has had on each of my children. And yet, I was so committed to the institution to marriage and "keeping the family together," that I ignored the glaring and obvious disfunction. You could say that I was becoming unhealthy as well. It was only after a good therapist and my support group, that I opened my eyes to *my* role.

When people say, "It takes two," they are right. It can be that one person in a marriage is cruel and selfish but if the other person allows it that person is reinforcing it by being enabling.

THREE

THE CONFLICT

I was slowing dying inside. There were times when my throat physically felt tight, as if I couldn't speak. Later on, I would recognize the absolute connection between my throat feeling strange and tight and that the fact that I wasn't being heard in my marriage.

To be perfectly clear, I would not have stayed with Wade if we didn't have kids. But I held on for them. To my very core, I bought into the belief that our children would suffer if we divorced. I believed that couples must stay together forever, and if divorce happens, the family will be torn apart in the afterlife. I decided I would do anything and everything I could not to let that happen.

While it is ideal that children have a mom and dad who are married, it isn't always possible. And for good reasons. A reason I had not considered up to that point was that I was showing my daughters how they should expect to be treated in a relationship. This came to me like a huge sock in the gut when I saw my oldest daughter, Brianna, allowing a young man she liked to treat her poorly. It was clear that he was playing emotional games with her, so I asked her, "Why do you allow him to treat you this way?"

As I was asking, it hit me. *She did this because this is what I do!*

···

FOUR

OUR NORMAL

We made many good memories, Wade and I, in spite of the thread of mental illness insidiously weaving itself around them. Moving to his hometown in Washington State brought us both challenging times and good times. Wade was quick-witted and had a keen sense of humor. He would improvise silly personalities that had us rolling in laughter! When his mood was high, he was a devoted husband. Wade used to tell me how wonderful I was and that I was smart and beautiful on a regular basis.

And he was a devoted dad. He came to every doctor's appointment with me during my pregnancy with each of our babies. He was also there to help catch them! As the kids got older, he attended every school performance, every sporting event that they played in, and every activity. I documented most of these with plenty of photographs. He loved to snuggle with each of our kids at bedtime.

He would play hide and seek with our son, Wes, at bedtime and hide under the covers. I would pretend not to know where they were and would call out, "Daddy . . . Wes . . . where are you?" I would pat the bed, and eventually, the game would end with tickles and lots of laughter.

Despite everything, we were plagued by Wade's mental illness.

Over twenty-two years, we met with many different therapists as a couple and as individuals. I recall one therapist describing Wade's cycling moods to me this way: Imagine a tire. Depending upon where you are on that tire, it is either good or unpleasant. The problem with the downturn of the tire is that you can get hurt. The more that the tire turns, the deeper the pain. And when the tire doesn't appear to be in the downturn, you still know it's coming. When you know it's coming, it's hard to trust the upturn of the tire (the good times).

The analogy made a lot of sense to me. On a warm summer morning, I recall Wade telling me, "Things are good. Just be happy." The problem was that he'd had a down mood swing just two days earlier. I became super untrusting of the "good times."

Wade had a serious addiction to escaping reality through screens—video games, social media, political chatrooms, and more. Every day he was on his screens. Withdrawing from the family was his normal behavior. What hurt me the most was that he wasn't fully present even when he was physically there. There were promises of improvement. Agreements were made and broken over and over again. We moved several times, looking for a new beginning. For a period, things seemed to improve, then the poisonous thread of mental illness would reveal itself again.

And yet, there were good times. We laughed, cried, loved, and created a family together. I did love Wade, and I know that he also loved me.

Together we decided that he would both pursue school and be the primary provider in our family. Before getting married, I had only attended some college and different trade schools. I lacked confidence in many ways. Thus, I felt comfortable with the thought that Wade would earn an income so I could stay home to raise our kids. I had always wanted to be a mom, yet I also had an entrepreneur's spirit. After I started a home-based business and began to earn some income of my own, my confidence increased exponentially.

My biggest regret looking back on those years is the memory of living with my eyes half-closed and not listening to my intuition. Ignoring my inner voice, I suffered from anxiety. When Wade was scary, I never called his behavior abuse. As I understood it, abuse involved physically harming someone. But he was emotionally abusive. I have since learned that this can cause the most damage.

Over the years, I would secretly wish that Wade would cheat on me so that I would be justified in filing for divorce. I never felt like I had a solid enough reason to leave him. I was also plagued with worry for his well-being. What would he do if I took the kids and left him? I recall feeling like he was my lost child and needed me to "fix him."

My commitment to finding a solution that would make the marriage workable led to several moves, Wade taking different types of medications, and career changes. I thought, *If I could do more, everything will work out. I can single-handedly save the family.*

Wade wasn't sick all the time. We had good times. We built businesses together. We shared the same entrepreneurial spirit. Ultimately, he was inspired to join a newly established multilevel-marketing essential oils company, and we built a business together that continues to sustain me.

We became so successful in this new business that at one point we were featured as emblems of leadership on the cover of the magazine *Networking Times.* Under our image, read the words "Can we have it all?" Truly we were blessed. Internal suffering, however, wasn't always visible on the outside. Within the walls of our home, there was a disconnect and even selfish behavior.

I contributed an article to that issue entitled "Raising Children and a Team."

Wade was good about taking me out weekly for a date night. He really did try to be a good husband. He wanted to be a loving husband and father. He loved me. He loved our kids! His healthy side was one of a fierce warrior. He would stand up for the underdog.

He had the ability to sense when things weren't right with one of our kids. If a child was struggling with an issue, he would bring it to light and help them through it. Later, I would learn he was correct.

Our relationship would ebb and flow. Looking back now, I recognize that the times when it wasn't good were the times when he was active in his addiction.

When I was a little girl, I imagined the perfect marriage. The perfect man. I believed marriage could be easy. I had hopes and dreams of feeling close to my husband. In my mind, he was tall, dark, handsome, and strong. He would take care of me. We would provide a loving and safe environment for our kids.

At intervals, I saw Wade make changes. He promised me that he had given up his addictions. I forgave him because I saw those demonstrable changes. For example, one of the worst incidences I can recall was the day I went down to the basement to ask him to come upstairs and help me in the kitchen. He didn't want to be interrupted, so he abruptly stood up and waved his middle finger in my face and cursed me to leave him alone. I was shocked. Realizing what he had done, he promised he wouldn't ever put his finger in my face or disconnect into the computer and video game world again.

He promised me. I would forgive him.

FIVE

....

SHAY

In February 2015, my oldest daughter, Brianna, married Shay, a young man whom we all adored. The week before the wedding was eventful. My two-year-old son broke his leg and was given a cast that extended well above his knee. Then, the day before the ceremony, Bri began feeling nauseous. It got so bad that Shay took her to the ER, where it was discovered that she had appendicitis. Her appendix needed to be removed immediately. During the procedure, the doctor found the presence of severe endometriosis, an overgrowth of uterine lining outside Bri's uterus. He scraped away much of this tissue, which he said would result in more painful recovery.

The doctor advised Bri not to leave the hospital for a few days to allow her to rest and heal. But she resisted this suggestion, stating, "I'm getting married, and I have to leave!" Within hours of surgery, on medication to help manage her surgical pain, she walked down the aisle.

With Shay's father, Karl, on her right and Wade on her left, Brianna walked very slowly down the aisle toward the altar. She made a beautiful bride. A dear friend of mine did her hair, which she wore in large curls draped over her shoulders. Another friend took candid photographs and video of the ceremony, which took place at an old, historic home in Provo, Utah.

The quaint building was reserved for special occasions like ours. In the front entry, there was a well-used wooden staircase that wound around, creating a picturesque place to pose. The main room seated up to seventy-five guests comfortably. A very large chandelier set off the space perfectly, creating a look of comfortable elegance. A small room off the main parlor had two long tables that held the soup and salad which were served for dinner.

The only thing not magical about the wedding reception was that Brianna couldn't dance.

There is a country song that always used to make Wade cry. The song talks about walking your little girl down the aisle and handing her off to her new husband. And of how the girl is "all grown up now." As the father of five daughters, you can imagine how this would resonate with a man like Wade. That moment would be bittersweet.

We were happy to welcome Shay into our midst. The instant he came into our lives, he was completely loved and part of our large family. He was fun-loving, kind, and wholesome. He had a heart of gold, which he wore on his sleeve. He fit right in.

Shay wore wire-rimmed glasses that always seemed to be sliding down his nose. He would push them up often. His chuckle and way of diffusing drama from the many girls in the family were downright adorable. He had the gift of love. He would wave at strangers and share his contagious smile with everyone he met. Shay also played with my little son for hours. He found sticks in the yard and role-played sword fighting with him.

One of the most endearing things Shay would do was to run and jump around barefoot outside. We joked with him that he looked much like a gazelle. Shay and Brianna loved the outdoors, so they often hiked and went camping. They got a puppy to share, Dexter. And Shay started taking family trips with us.

Our trip to southern California was memorable. Shay had never been to the beach, and he saw the ocean for the first time. Living out west in the desert of Utah, trips to the ocean are a rarity. It was an unusually cold and windy day. The wind blew hard. We brought all kinds of snacks with us, both food and drinks. Blankets were laid out. Everyone eagerly dressed in a swimsuit and timidly walked toward the rushing waves. The water was ice cold, and the waves were strong. I took video and photos from the beach. They laughed and shrieked.

They came in to get some snacks, shivering in their wet suits. We naively began to feed the seagulls and very soon found ourselves surrounded by hundreds of screaming birds flying toward us to catch a bite of food. It was overwhelming, to say the least. It wasn't the perfect beach experience, but it is one that I will cherish forever. It is a beautiful memory.

Another family trip that included Shay was a trip to Arches National Park in Moab, Utah. It was later the same season and quite warm outside. As we hiked, Shay carried our boy on his shoulders. I took loads of photos to document these special moments. Standing barefoot, he encouraged our daughters to climb the deep red rocks with unusual shapes. Laughter was heard.

Shay was part of our family. We loved him. We accepted him.

Brianna and Shay met through his mom, who worked with Brianna at our local bakery. He was young and olive-skinned with the thickest head of hair. His biological father came from Mexico. Shay didn't really know him because the man left when he was just a baby.

Shay was raised by his mother and stepdad, Karl, whom she had wed when Shay was very young. Karl was a father to Shay and adored him.

There were no warning signs that Shay was in deep trouble. At least not signs that I picked up on. It seemed to come out of the blue.

Just nine months into his marriage to Brianna, Shay began to experience deep episodes of depression. Help was offered, and yet his behavior became more erratic. Brianna expressed so much concern and wasn't sure what to do. She knew him. We knew him! This wasn't "him." The day he disappeared left us so deeply upset that neither food nor sleep was had by anyone. They'd had a simple disagreement. Calls and voicemails were left on his phone. Begging and pleading for him to return to us continued. It was impossible not to let our fear get the best of us. The worry ran very deep because it was December and cold outside.

As a family and community of friends, we frantically searched for him. It was a bitterly cold winter. He was such a young man and they had only been married ten short months. Posters were hung around local shops with his name and photo. Multiple messages were left on his phone from the entire family. Brianna pleaded with him through voicemail to come back home, saying that she loved him.

The morning I heard the knock at our front door I was brought to my knees. It had been five days since her husband left when a police officer knocked on the door, asking for Brianna. Fearing the worst, I asked, "Is it Shay? Did something happen to him?"

The policeman reluctantly told me that Shay had been found dead in Rock Springs, Wyoming, from a self-inflicted gunshot wound to the head.

A few moments later, my daughter and her dad walked in the front door. Wade and Brianna had been out driving around to the places where the couple liked to camp, looking for signs of Shay. Immediately upon hearing the news, Bri ran into the guest bathroom off the living room and began to heave into the toilet. She fell to her knees. I came behind her and scooped her up in my arms as I did when she was a small child. Her head rested on my chest, and I braced her upright by the shoulders. She then collapsed into my lap completely. She was shaking and sobbing loudly.

As I held Bri next to the cool porcelain toilet bowl, I looked around. A large mirror hung above the vanity. The floor beneath us was old-style linoleum. The walls were painted forest green with a white baseboard. I took in my surroundings as some sort of escape from the shocking news.

The news didn't feel real. The swirl of reactions to the tragedy spread like wildfire throughout the entire family. Screaming and wailing was heard from upstairs and in the other rooms on the ground floor. After Brianna got up and splashed some cold water on her face, we went back to the living room where the police officer informed us that Shay had stolen a gun from a small gun shop in Wyoming, after which he located a deserted construction site where he shot himself.

The thoughts of those first few moments after hearing these details haunt me to this day. It was well below freezing and Shay must have been without proper warmth as he sat there alone, waiting to decide to exit this life. The coroner estimated that he had passed away in the early morning hours.

Shay was a twenty-year-old young man for whom we cared deeply. He laughed with us. He loved us. We loved him. Our lives would be different from that moment on.

Wade and Brianna drove to Rock Springs to pick up Shay's few belongings from the police station. When the day-long roundtrip finally came to an end, Wade walked into the house and broke down in tears. He showed me the glasses that Shay wore, which had been badly broken by the gunshot, then turned his head downward, sobbingly loudly.

SIX

....

DEEP GRIEF

Brianna and Shay had purchased their first home and remodeled it themselves. Many memories had been made of the entire family painting it, tearing out the old carpet, and updating the lights and hardware. Shay's father, Karl, had replaced the air conditioning unit. Brianna would now be living alone in this home.

The days and weeks after Shay's passing were excruciating for me. I felt helpless to comfort my grieving daughter. How much I wanted to cradle her in my arms and erase her pain!

Heaps of Shay's clothes and other belongings were a continual reminder to Bri that her husband was gone. The clothing was scattered about because she had been rummaging through the drawers and closets a few days before in an effort to find a clue as to where he had gone. He had taken their camping supplies with him: a tent, a sleeping bag, and premade meals intended for outdoor survival.

A small safe turned up that normally would have contained a pair of tiny diamond earrings that were a gift to Brianna from her grandfather on her eighteenth birthday. They were gone. Shay had apparently taken whatever he could that had value before he left. It is evident that he wasn't thinking clearly.

Looking back on her husband behavior recently, my daughter told me that she now recognizes that he was displaying warning signs of mental illness. He was plagued by depression. As far back as when they originally met, he had said he felt very depressed and intended to leave this earth. He also told her that he didn't because of her.

Shay's moods would cycle much like those of my husband. There were many happy times, but the happiness wasn't consistent. It felt almost fragile—like the couple was walking on eggshells. From the outside, all appeared normal. Underneath, there was an addiction to gaming, unresolved issues, and pain.

Concern for Brianna's safety was ever-present and utmost in my mind. I could see her making poor choices to regulate her pain. She was trying to numb out with alcohol, for instance, which I feared because she is diabetic and needed to monitor her blood sugar carefully. That is a dangerous combination.

Brianna shared that she could feel Shay standing behind her in spirit during her darkest hours. "It was so real, Mom," she said. "I could feel him. It was as if he was telling me to stop spiraling down."

My daughter has always been a lover of all animals. She would rescue all kinds of little critters growing up. She is sensitive and kind and takes the best care of God's creations. A couple of times a week, I would help her clean her little animal cages. Taking care of her animals was quite therapeutic for Bri.

I encouraged her. I prayed for her. I was at her home continually. She was determined to stay in her home. "It is all I have from Shay, Mom," she would tell me. My daughter was in unbearable emotional pain, so I began buying her things in an effort somehow to make it better. Daily phone calls to check on her were necessary.

One morning I was unable to reach her by phone. I called and called. No answer. I decided to drive to her home. I knocked on the front door and got no answer. I tried the door handle. It was locked. I began knocking on the front windows while I continued to call her. Fear got the best of me, and I began to yell the best I could through the front door.

My heart pounded from the thought I had lost my daughter. She was never suicidal, as far as I know, but she was in the depths of darkness and expressed upon occasion that she didn't want to live sometimes because the pain was so awful.

To my relief, Brianna finally opened her front door. I hugged her tightly and told her how worried I'd been. She apologized and said she had just fallen asleep.

Getting through the crisis of grief was a day-by-day, hour-by-hour proposition. My focus was not only on helping her heal emotionally but on physically keeping her with us.

Bri was under attack on many fronts. She endured blame and even threats from a couple of people on her husband's side of the family. During those very dark times, I reassured her that those people were just hurting and didn't know how to process Shay's passing—that their feelings were misdirected. It wasn't until much later on, after sincere apologies from those individuals, that she truly understood my reassurance.

Somehow the sun still rose and set.

Tender mercies wove through the excruciating pain.

At the one-year anniversary of Bri and Shay's marriage, two months after his passing, Wade posted a message on Facebook, along with the photo of himself tying Shay's tie. He wrote:

Shay, we are really missing you this week. I wish I would have told you I loved you more, how much I appreciated you more. Sometimes we think folks will be around forever, and then they are not. I loved tying your tie, buddy. I never told you that. I remember you were a bit embarrassed you didn't know how to tie a tie. All that did is make me love you more. You were just like me and didn't like to ask for help. (Kind of a guy thing too). I wish we could have helped you more. You were a good man, Shaylor! I miss you.

One afternoon Wade and I snuck away for quiet time together at our favorite restaurant. As we sat across from each other, I shared with him that I longed to testify to the power of prayer and spread the message that none of us are alone in our heartache. That healing is available. I told him, "I sense this is part of my mission on earth."

Later that day, as I was reading, I ran across a quote that spoke to me which reiterated my sentiment. I hung it on my mirror, where to this day it is still held up by a small piece of Scotch tape. It is a bit worn looking and faded now after the move I subsequently made to a new house, but I kind of like that.

This quote from religious scholar and church leader Jeffery R. Holland has brought me great comfort over the ensuing years.

> I testify of angels, both the heavenly and the mortal kind. In doing so I am testifying that God never leaves us alone, never unaided in the challenges that we face. . . . Always there are those angels who come and go all around us, seen and unseen, known and unknown, mortal and immortal.[1]

....

SEVEN

MISTRUST, FEAR, AND TRAUMA

Two short months after Shay's passing, I received a text from Wade in which he informed me that his life wasn't worth much anymore and he had done his best. I got this message, sounding much like a suicide threat, as I was driving to my sister's in our large Suburban Wagon with four of the kids.

We'd planned a family get-together that day with our kids at my sister's home, which was twenty minutes away. At the last minute, Wade decided he wasn't going to come with us. This made me really angry because I knew he was going to be at home, diddling around on the computer or playing videos games.

It was embarrassing. I didn't want to have to apologize for his absence to my sister or cover for Wade. I wanted him with me. I really wanted to be a family and feel his presence and support. I wanted him to hold my hand. I wanted him to help with our kids and be involved. The feeling of disconnection felt so bad, and yet it was familiar.

I was so mad that I confronted him. I raised my voice as I told him, "You don't support me. You are so uninvolved in our lives because you are addicted to screens and to escaping. Do you not understand how important it is to me that you come with me?"

I slammed the door on my way out of the house.

I was in such a huff that I asked Brianna to drive. Thankfully, I was in the front passenger seat when I got the text message because it really shook me up.

I immediately tried to call Wade. No answer. I tried calling again. No answer. I imagined the worst: coming home to find him dead in our garage. My thoughts went to: *What guns do we have in the house? Will he find the key to the safe where they're kept?* My legs began to shake, my heart raced, and I felt impending doom.

I texted again and again. "Please," I begged, "tell me you're safe. Remember the agreement, the 'safety plan' we made with our therapist. Please just tell me you're safe! If you need alone time, that is fine. But I am scared." No response.

Finally, he texted me back. "All is well."

It didn't bring me much comfort.

The minutes seemed like hours as we continued the trek to my sister's house, with my kids not knowing the worry that now consumed me.

When we arrived, I reached out to a friend of Wade's by phone. I begged him to drive to our home and make sure Wade was OK. He agreed he would. Then I waited and waited, fearing the worst-case scenario.

As I sat in the Suburban, after what felt like an hour, I heard from his friend. He dialed me as he was walking into our home. He began calling out, "Wade, Wade, Wade? Are you here?" He told me he saw a light on upstairs and made his way up the stairs toward the room with the light on. Wade was there, seated in his computer chair, pretending to be asleep.

The friend explained that I was worried and asked Wade why he didn't call me. He said he was tired and "must have fallen asleep." I was sure this was a lie.

"Don't keep guns in your home," his therapist told me after I recounted the story to him.

"Where should I put the key to the gun safe?" I asked him.

"At a different location," he told me.

Secretly, I gave my sister the key, which she kept at her house well hidden.

A few weeks later, I had heard what seemed like gunshots outside our home within a hundred yards. Wade came up to me and said he needed the key to the safe where we kept our guns, as he'd heard the same sounds. He wanted to be able to defend us if necessary. My heart went into my throat, and my stomach dropped to the floor. I was silent at first because I didn't want to tell him that the key wasn't there. Then I quickly explained that I was following the advice of the therapist who had told me not to keep it near the safe anymore.

Wade began to yell at me. He swore. He cursed the therapist. As he did this, I felt myself getting stronger in that realization that he did, indeed, need help, and it was not my fault.

Wade went on like this for forty-five minutes. "Please stop yelling," I told him. "You will regret the things you say right now."

Sure enough, later that day he did apologize for his behavior after we discovered that the sounds that we'd heard were just our neighbors target shooting in their barn.

Mistrust, fear, and trauma were such a part of my daily life that I had become detached from more ordinary concerns, like what to make for dinner.

EIGHT

....

CALIFORNIA

We were sorting through Grandpa's things: dishes, vases, old photos, clothing, and shoes. My mom's father had passed away just weeks before. She deeply missed him. Grandpa had a shed on his property in northern California. We placed two folding chairs in it, sat down, and sorted. I treasured this time with my mom and sister, Raquel, who is twenty years younger than me. My mom gave birth to her after my parents divorced. Her arrival was a blessing from heaven. She has Down syndrome and often talks about very spiritual things, which at times catches me off guard and brings tears to my eyes! After Shay's passing, she talked a lot about him being with our Father in heaven and how he is serving him.

We were up to our elbows in dust and overwhelmed by the sheer magnitude of the stuff Grandpa had collected. Things were being organized in sections to be prepared for the estate sale. We were grateful for the warm spring weather. Mom was so happy to find some old ancestor photos. She is an avid genealogist. I have fond memories of visiting cemeteries with her and going over the words lightly with chalk to be able to read the birth and death dates. She did her research while raising eight children close in age. After a full day of sorting, we had a meal at a local restaurant. Then we took photos next to the lake in the town. We documented the day to honor my grandfather.

You learn a lot about people when you go through their belongings. Grandpa was a good man with a few quirks. He also was meticulous about his things. He had served in Vietnam, and we came across an album full of graphic pictures from the war. I'd had no idea about the terrible things he had seen as a soldier or the pain he must have felt because of it! He had married several times and divorced. Finally, he found Diane, the love of his life. He and Diane had a beautiful connection and marriage of many years. But Grandpa changed after she got sick with cancer and died. He was lonely, so he got a dog.

My parents adopted his very sweet dog after his passing.

I wish I could say that the trip to clean out Grandpa's house was blissful, but that would be far from the truth because of what was going on back at home with Wade and my children. Before I left home, Wade made agreements with me around his screen time and his involvement in the routines of the family. He agreed not to be on screens after 5 PM. While I was in California, I received a text from one of my daughters, letting me know that he was not honoring his promises. He was playing computer games well into the night, and the younger kids were dirty, the house was a mess, and chores were not being done. Our daughter was unaware of the agreement. She just felt worried.

I phoned our couples therapist, a professional we had chosen as a last resort. "What do I do?" I asked her. She told me that things between Wade and I needed to be transparent if we were to succeed at saving our marriage. In other words, I should phone and discuss his behavior with him.

I just "knew" the trouble was all Wade's fault. If he could just make some changes, then we would work. At that point, I didn't understand my role in our marital dynamic. I was an angry enabler.

So, the call was made to Wade. "Why are you breaking our agreement?" I asked him. He denied it completely and became very angry at our daughter.

As I sat outside my grandpa's house, I was in emotional turmoil. My stomach was in knots. Anxiety filled my entire being. My daughter got on the telephone. "Why did you tell Dad that I told you this?" she asked. She was mad at me now because he was furious with her.

The argument that day escalated to the point that he was threatening to leave the house. I begged him to stay until I got back. The kids had school and with younger kids to watch and a house to run, he needed to be there to fulfill his parental responsibilities.

Our therapist called him in for an intervention session. She promised she would call me afterward so I could speak safely in private with her, she said.

During the intervention, which I attended remotely on speakerphone, while they met in person in her office, I told Wade that he was "my hardest child." He was indeed not keeping his commitments, and quite frankly, I was fed up.

Then I vented. Why was I worried about him and his emotions continually? I truly felt that I was raising a big, immature, selfish boy.

In response to everything I said, he told me he was getting an apartment and leaving immediately. "Our daughter needs to put on her big girl britches, watch the kids, and take care of things in the household until you get back," he told me.

After much discussion, including input from the therapist, he changed his mind and agreed to stay until I got back the next day.

I returned home late the following evening as my flight from California was delayed. Nobody was awake when I arrived. I knew what I was coming home to. I had felt this familiar feeling before—like I was being manipulated to give Wade attention. I was very, very angry and disgusted. I crawled into bed, putting ample distance between my body and Wade's, and fell asleep.

The next morning, I awoke to excited kids welcoming me home. In my marriage, I felt that I was the "glue." If at times I was sick or gone even for a few hours, things would fall apart. This was much more than the typical thing that most moms gripe about. I literally felt as if I held everything in the household together. I needed to be the strong one, to keep the peace. Beyond loving me, my children craved stability, which was why they'd missed me so much.

There were conversations when I would ask Wade, "When do I get to be tired or weak?" Not that I wanted to be, but I wanted to feel safe and be taken care of occasionally! Between severe depression, neck and back pain, anxiety, lack of energy, and self-destructive behavior, Wade always had something to focus on, a thing that was rarely me. This might have rewarded me at some point by making me feel important. But it had worn thin.

Now, I can recognize that I did this to myself. I played a key role in our unhealthy, codependent relationship. To this day, it is my biggest regret that I was such a classic enabler. I can see the very damaging effect it has had on each of my children. And yet, I was so committed to the institution to marriage and the idea of "keeping the family together" that I ignored our glaring and obvious dysfunction.

You could say that I was as unhealthy as Wade, or at least becoming so. It has only been after working individually with a good therapist for a few years and with the help of a peer support group that I finally opened my eyes to my role in our drama.

When people say, "It takes two to tango," they are right. Even if one person is cruel and selfish, the other person allows it and reinforces it by enabling.

NINE

······································

CONFERENCE WEEKEND
APRIL 2, 2016

I decided to attend a church conference in Salt Lake City on the morning following my trip to California to clean out my grandfather's house. Brianna and her friend Jack came with me. Or more precisely, I attended with them. Bri was able to get tickets to this special annual event and had invited me to attend with her. I carefully considered the situation when I awoke. My concern over my daughter and the loss she'd suffered were what propelled me to go and put having a serious discussion with Wade on the back burner. Before I drove off, the tension between us was thick and oppressive. Wade was agitated. "I'll be home about 1 PM," I told him.

During the two-hour church session in which we listened to inspiring messages from important leaders of our church, I prayed fervently in my heart for divine instruction. I really don't recall what else I got from the service other than reassurance that I was not alone.

As we made our way out of the large conference center, my mind was swirling with thoughts of what I knew I needed to do back home, which was to confront Wade. I felt nervous. The drive home would be about one hour.

Just as Bri, Jack, and I were getting on the freeway heading south, I received an urgent phone call. All three of us could hear everything as the call came via a hands-free connection. My fifteen-year-old daughter, Alyssa's, voice, was so shaky that I could hardly understand her. She began to scream, "Mom, Dad is going to kill himself. Help me, please. I don't know what to do!"

Firmly, I turned and told Brianna to dial 9-1-1.

As Bri was answering the first few questions from the dispatcher, I asked Alyssa what Wade was doing at that moment. My thoughts went to the previous months and the conversations with therapists about guns. The same dreadful feeling I'd had before I hid the key to the safe overtook me again.

My heart raced as Alyssa informed me, "He is dressed in a church suit, Mom. He's acting strange and crying. And he told me that his life isn't worth living anymore, but that mine was.

"I cried, Mom, and asked him, 'What are you talking about? Are you going to kill yourself?' Mom, I'm scared!"

My head whirled with all kinds of horrible images. I could feel my heart racing in my chest, and my stomach ached. My legs felt weak. With Jack in the back seat and Brianna in the front passenger seat, I drove as quickly as I could, weaving in and out of construction cones and lane changes. I recall a prayer being offered out loud.

I insisted that the 9-1-1 dispatcher send an ambulance to the house, fearing that Wade had taken something. Soon after he discovered I had hidden the key to the gun safe, he'd told me, "Hiding the key is useless. If I really wanted to kill myself, I have all the pills I need to do so."

Arriving home, we saw that there were several cop cars and an ambulance parked on the property. I was in a rush to speak with them. They needed to know the seriousness of the situation. We met them collectively outside the house as I pulled halfway into the driveway. Shaking, I told them, "Please, you need to understand. My son-in-law committed suicide just a few months ago. He can't do it, too! My kids! We couldn't make it. This would be too hard! Please, you have to help us."

The police on the scene informed me that Wade seemed OK and was calm. He had told them that he was wearing a suit because he was doing laundry and had nothing else clean to wear. "He has appointments and plans this week," they said. "We can't take him against his will."

"Please, officers," I begged. "He doesn't wear suits, and he isn't OK."

"Let us get a crisis worker on the phone," they said. I assented.

After a few moments of speaking with the police, they put me on the call. The crisis worker began asking me questions. She said, "Technically, since he is over eighteen and seems fine, and had a logical explanation for his behavior—that he has appointments scheduled for this coming week—we can't do anything."

Desperately, I said again, "Please, help! He isn't OK. We cannot have another suicide in the family!" Honestly, I couldn't tell if his actions were his typical attention-seeking behavior or if he really intended to leave this earth. Either way, I was tired. The situation had me in over my head, and it was causing irreparable damage.

The crisis worker agreed to speak with the police again on my behalf.

It was then that the police noticed a paper in Wade's front shirt pocket. I sat on the front porch swing. He was inside with the cops and refusing to show them the paper.

As the situation was unfolding, I called my sister to come to get my younger kids. They didn't need to witness the drama. The older kids remained at home.

I felt as if I were merely a witness to the situation at hand. This didn't feel like my life. *I did it all right! Why is this happening to ME?* I thought. I had tried to keep the family together. If I did right and "endured to the end," wouldn't my reward be a happy and eternal family? Wouldn't that mean I would be happy, and Wade would be healed? Things had to get better! I just knew I would receive rewards and blessings from staying true to my marriage promise.

"I can reach him," I told the police. "He loves me, and he will do this for me, right?" So, I entered the house and pleaded with him, "Please, can I see the paper in your pocket?"

He replied, "No."

I looked into his eyes through tears and begged, "You are scaring me, Wade. Please let me have the paper to see what it says."

He then informed me, "This is between me and another party."

I knew then. The police knew too. It was as if the emotional string between us, our marriage bond, snapped at that moment. There was zero trust in his eyes. For years there had always been glimmers of trust, so I hung on. I'd hung on for the kids. I hadn't wanted to put my kids through a divorce.

And I didn't want to come to regret leaving either. I had heard statistics of second marriages not working out. I saw firsthand my parents' divorce. There was regret, and then after twenty-four years, they remarried. *This will be me,* I had told myself.

Or I mused, *He will marry some other lady and be wonderful to her! Why did I get the crap end of the deal?* I created such stories out of fear. My fear had clouded my vision, which is why I'd ignored my gut feelings about Wade's behavior over and over again.

Living with someone with mental health issues is a completely different ballgame than a marriage between two mentally healthy adults. There are times when what's happening doesn't make sense. Trying to make sense out of my marriage wasn't about it being "perfect" because, as you know, no marriage is. It was about the poison that had resulted in root rot. We were dying as a couple from the inside. Our roots were rotten. Trust was gone.

The demeanor of the police officer in charge of the scene changed as he began to believe me. Now everyone could see that Wade was a danger to himself. Going back and forth seemed to take about forty-five minutes. The standoff came to an end when they informed Wade that because he was refusing to show them the paper in his pocket, they could only assume it was a suicide letter. That would be the reason they would need to take him in against his will.

Wade begged, "Please don't cuff me in front of my kids."

I was struck by, and will always remember, the very sick look Wade gave me as he was walking past me with a policeman behind him. I was seated on the wooden porch swing and in turmoil. Just a few steps from the front door, he turned and shook his head at me as if in disgust.

He was safely in the police car when I walked slowly into the house. Inside, I collapsed onto the wooden bench in the kitchen. I then sent my older kids to get lunch, mostly so they could escape the oppressive drama. As soon as they were gone, I sobbed out loud. I screamed. I couldn't recognize the kinds of sounds that were coming out of my mouth. Thankfully I was alone and didn't have to pretend I was all right.

I knew what this incident meant. It meant that it would be only a matter of time before I would be planning Wade's funeral. He wasn't safe. I couldn't trust him.

I continued to wail. This man had been mine for twenty-two years. We had shared our dreams, our passions, our fears. I thought he would be the one I grew old with. I had thought we would share grandkids. My grief was a deep river.

I had time alone, and I welcomed it. I am quite sure that I had help from the other side in these moments because even during the emotional blackness, I noticed the brightness of the sun. The warmth felt good, and I felt safe. It was a warm spring day. I noticed the buds on the trees as I looked out of the kitchen window.

A bit later, there was a knock at the door. It was a policeman asking to talk to me. He was one of just a few officers who had been on the scene. The town where we lived was small, and I knew that he was a good man, a family man. This kind man began to apologize to me for not listening to me immediately and thanked me over and over for insisting that they take my concerns seriously. He had come to inform me that the letter Wade was carrying in his pocket was indeed a suicide note. The man asked me if I wanted a copy of it and I quickly said no. I knew I couldn't stomach reading it right then.

In fact, Wade had written a letter to each of us explaining why he had left this earth. Many months later, I would muster the courage to request those letters from the police department.

At last, I could see clearly that my husband had a mental illness, and I understood that allowing this madness to continue in our home was hurting the kids.

I was angry. I had been walking a fine line with Wade that was very difficult to walk. I'd walked the same line off and on for years. However, this was farthest he had taken his threats. Now he had to go. I knew that Wade could not come home again.

TEN

··

THE HOSPITAL STAY

The days following Wade's detention were filled with turmoil. *He cannot come home. How can I tell him this? What will he do?*

The man I arranged for Wade to stay with when he was released from custody was a casual friend, someone whom Wade would see a movie or get lunch with on occasion. He assured me that he would do his best to ensure Wade was safe. As someone who had threatened to kill himself, Wade would need to be watched closely.

Just nine short days later, on Sunday morning, I received a call from the mental health hospital informing me that it was time for Wade to leave. They said he seemed to be doing OK and that he should continue to be seen by a therapist. He was scheduled to be released the next day.

"Does it have to be this way?" I asked the administrator. It felt as if I had knots in my stomach, and my legs were limp noodles. I was filled with anxiety. I kept envisioning the worst-case scenario in my mind over and over. That he got home and took his life.

I felt like I had a complete lack of control over the situation. Heaviness hung in the air.

Late in the afternoon, Brianna got a phone call from her dad, who began saying some of the same things he had told Alyssa on the day the police had to escort him out of the house. Devasted by what she heard, she called me. Her voice was shaking. "Mom, I think Dad is going to kill himself. He can't get out. They can't let him leave!" she said.

My daughter had buried her husband just a few months before. To call her experience *trauma* doesn't even give it proper justice.

In my opinion, when people make phone calls such as the one that Wade made to our daughter, they are seeking attention. It is an unhealthy manipulation done to feed some void in their psyche. This was not the first time her dad had expressed himself in this manner. He had been doing it throughout his life. Back in 1993, before he met me, a girl he was going out with rejected him. In an attempt to get her attention, he took an entire bottle of over-the-counter sleeping pills. He then phoned her and said, "I feel weird. I just took some pills." She called 9-1-1. An ambulance showed up and took him to the hospital, where he had his stomach pumped. Because he was over eighteen and didn't want to stay, they let him leave after a few hours.

I only learned of this story from his sister a few weeks before his death, and it helped me make sense of so much. We began unhealthily. He had been unable to cope with rejection and was looking to me to "complete" him. Because I had longed to create the perfect happy family, I ignored my gut instincts, which were telling me something was wrong.

In therapy, I have learned that a healthy relationship is built on trust. Trust comes from being able to predict your partner's behavior—how he will act within a certain scale of reactions. When you cannot predict behavior in a relationship, you feel like you are tiptoeing around, and this causes resentment to build.

In my marriage with Wade, anger and unmet needs became who I was. I was suffering. He was never physically abusive with me or any of our children. The damage came from him isolating himself, his unpredictable mood swings, and his manipulative, attention-seeking behavior. It always felt like there was a cloud of chaos surrounding him.

With some effort, I got hold of his therapist from the hospital and insisted that they keep him there longer. They agreed to delay the release for two days.

On the day of his release, I met Wade at the exit interview with the friend with whom he would be staying. The room was small and uninviting. It held a small desk with a computer. The chairs were metal with plastic seats. I felt cold. The whole situation was surreal. Wade and I had shared half of our lives, and yet it felt as awkward to be with him as if I were sitting with a stranger.

Wade began to talk about his plans for coming home, but I interrupted to tell him, "You are not coming home."

"I'm not?" he replied. "I need to at least come over to pack."

"I packed for you," I said. "The stuff you need is all at your friend's house already."

Wade squirmed in his chair and looked disappointed. I felt terrible—like I was kicking my child to the curb. It was foreign for me to say no to him.

The discussion between us went on for about an hour. He seemed genuinely surprised when I explained,

"I'm so mad at you, Wade. How could you do this to us? To our kids? How could you, especially after all the trauma and loss we experienced with Shay? You have caused permanent damage, and things won't ever be the same."

His eyes were wide with a look of shock and derangement. I could see the mental illness in them. I couldn't recognize this man.

ELEVEN

....

AN ANGELIC VISITOR

Late one night, about a month after Wade's suicide attempt was foiled, I was lying awake in my bed worrying. The kids were fast asleep. I started praying out loud to my heavenly Father. "Father, how can I bear so much trauma? What if he dies too? This family has had so much loss. I need help."

I also prayed for the assistance of angels, and I got very specific in my asking. I knew that the more specific my requests were, the more specifically they would be answered. Someone once told me to imagine prayer as being comparable to going to a drive-through window and placing an order. If I asked for just "food," I might not get exactly what I wanted. However, if I asked for my favorite salad with an extra dressing and a favorite side dish, I would receive that.

So, I asked. I begged. Tears soaked my pillow. I prayed that Wade would be healed. I prayed that he would be safe. I begged for healing for each of my kids. I felt tremendous worry and pain, but at the same time, I also felt I was being heard. I began to feel the presence of a spiritual being hovering just above my body, and I was filled with so much peace. I was told, "He will not be taken until it is his time." The message wasn't in words. It came to my mind telepathically, for lack of a better description.

I don't remember anything else that happened that night because I fell fast asleep. When I woke up the next morning, I felt peaceful and calm. The experience stuck with me over the coming months. I would trust. Our lives were in God's hands.

That spring, I attended my first women's betrayal trauma group. When I was invited, I didn't think the group applied to me. Reluctantly, I went. The meeting was held in someone's home. It was quite beautiful. A very large, fluffy couch caught my eye, and I grabbed a seat. Chairs were placed close to several other pieces of major furniture to form a circle. As women began filing in, I awkwardly smiled and made eye contact with each one. They all looked kind and a little bit like me. Some acted more confident, and it was apparent that this was not their first time attending. A few very friendly women came over and introduced themselves to me.

One woman took charge of the group and welcomed all who attended. There was a type of memorized quote that the women began to recite. It reminded me of the Serenity Prayer that I had heard many years earlier while teaching yoga at a drug and alcohol treatment center:

God, grant me the serenity to accept the things I cannot change,

Courage to change the things I can,
And wisdom to know the difference.[2]

Then the sharing began. Until then, I hadn't thought that the meeting applied to my situation. However, within minutes, I began to relate to each woman as she shared her experiences. I was brought to tears. Up to that very moment, my focus had been on everything Wade was doing wrong. *If only he would change this or that, stop doing this or that, if only he would treat me better and stop being selfish, THEN everything would be OK. We could be happy!* Now it became apparent to me that I had played a role. I had allowed myself to be treated poorly. I had allowed Wade's behavior to continue in our home. I had not held the boundaries I established. I finally understood! Because I had swept Wade's mental illness under the carpet, what was completely dysfunctional became our normal.

I still loved him! And yet, I could see things clearly. I could see how staying with him hurt my kids.

Spiritually, I was being given what I needed at the time I needed it. Messages were showing up for me, and I couldn't deny that they were inspired or specifically for me!

With a surge of power that felt like a direct message from heaven, I wrote the following message on a small whiteboard and placed it on my dresser in my bedroom.

I must be a strong, stable parent. I must take care of myself. I must show my kids that I keep my word. I must not compromise the principles of righteousness. I must release what does not bring me JOY.

I never did erase that whiteboard. To this day, the message on it is my constant reminder that I won't ever be alone and that my happiness matters to me and to all those I love.

The following months were filled with anxiety, fear, and deep pain. My health was affected. At one point, I even wondered if I have a serious health issue. My stomach hurt all the time. My appetite left me. I knew what I wanted and needed to do—divorce Wade—and yet I was scared. How I longed for an angel to appear and just tell me what to do!

Praying *Do I divorce?* my answer was as clear as the breath of life is in me, "Not now."

....

TWELVE

THE LAST TIME
I SAW WADE

Wade and I met for a two-hour therapy session on August 10. During the session, I told him that I wasn't filing for divorce yet. I agreed to give it time. But I also told him that he had to give me a full disclosure of his behavior. I suspected that he had struggled with an addiction to pornography, and he now admitted this to me. Finally. For years I had wanted to believe that he was just addicted to video games. Much time had been wasted negotiating with him to play them less or not at all. For years I felt angry! Now I knew that he never listened to me. He didn't hear my pleading!

Addiction is the ultimate mechanism for separation.

I wanted him—all of him! I didn't want to share him with addictions anymore. I didn't want to compete for his love. My heart ached. It was broken.

And there was something else going on that I couldn't quite put my finger on. I didn't quite believe him when he gave the disclosure of his betrayals of me. For this reason, I decided I couldn't let him come back home yet. If ever. I had just set a healthy boundary—finally.

The next day, at approximately 6 PM, Wade took over-the-counter sleeping pills. He purposefully did this right before his friend would arrive home from work. He wanted to be discovered and rescued. While fully dressed, he climbed into the bathtub, where he fell asleep with the water running. But Wade's friend had a dinner date that evening that Wade didn't know about and did not arrive home until 9 PM. At that point, the water had flooded his home. Knowing something wasn't right, he ran through the house yelling for Wade. No response. Following the sound of the running water, he entered the bathroom and discovered my husband in the tub. It was too late to save him.

The cause of death was drowning.

THIRTEEN

....

I RECEIVED THE CALL

I received notification of Wade's death while watching Michael Phelps victoriously swimming a race during the 2016 Summer Olympics. My parents' home was abuzz with family cheering on the Olympic swimmers. We had just finished dinner. My entire family was in town, and Wade had begged to come to the reunion. But as I had told him the day before, I wasn't ready for that.

In retrospect, there were signs of heavenly protection around me that evening. Just minutes before the phone call, my baby nephew started giving me hugs—something he hadn't done before. I marveled at the love he was showing me. My parents' dog was also paying special attention to me, and she hadn't done that before! I had just spoken with my dad concerning the therapy session the day before.

I answered my phone. "Hello?" It was my daughter Alyssa telling me that a cop was at our house, and he needed to talk to me "in person." "I knew what this meant. My heart began to race. Then my legs went weak, and I fell to the floor.

I kept saying, "No, no, no!"

Seeing how upset I was, in an urgent tone, my brother asked me, "Laura, what's wrong?" He began screaming it when I didn't reply. "Are your kids OK? What is going on?"

I pulled myself together and asked the policeman on the other end of the line, "Tell me what happened. Is he gone? Is he dead?"

The policeman replied, "I need to talk to you in person."

I begged, "Please tell me . . . I'm with my entire family."

Reluctantly, he told me, "Yes, he is gone."

I immediately collapsed into a heap in my parents' living room. In some strange way, I was able to witness myself screaming and crying out, "My kids, my kids!" My sister held me just as I'd held my daughter eight months earlier.

I lay in the fetal position sobbing, my head in my sister's lap. I was in shock. This was so surreal. What I had dreaded happening had happened. I was living a nightmare! My recollections are a jumble. I recall the comforting sensation as my sister brushed my hair away from my face. And I have a slight memory of my father giving me a blessing within minutes. He said, "You will have a joy that you have never known." That was a promise. A tender mercy from God that would sustain me.

Brianna picked up Caitlyn, Alyssa, and Emma, and drove them from our house to my parent's house. We needed to be together. That first evening was filled with shock. I listened to my kids crying. I knew one of my daughters was in my parent's bathroom, sobbing. Everyone and everything seemed to be swirling around me, and I couldn't absorb much detail. I called Wade's mom and told her what had happened. That her only son had passed. I could hear her voice shake as she took in the news.

My youngest daughter was playing with her cousins in the playroom in my parents' basement with no idea of what was happening upstairs. I knew that I would need to tell her. She was summoned to come to see me. This child is so kind and sweet. Telling her that her Daddy had passed was almost too much to bear. Her face lowered, and she began to cry quietly.

My son was just three years old, and he had now lost not only his brother-in-law, whom he saw as an older brother but also his dad. I could tell he didn't understand what happened. He studied my upset face and hugged me.

My soul ached, and I felt myself detach from the physical realm. It must have been some sort of protection, as the pain was so much to bear.

My mom made makeshift beds for me and my six children in the living room using sleeping bags and blankets from her storage room. We wanted to be together. The night was spent tossing and turning, but mostly I remember the shock.

Would there be no end to the grieving? I was stepping into another place of being. My world would no longer be the same. I had been in the refiner's fire for nearly a full year beginning with the loss of Shay, and yet the hottest, most difficult fire had always been waiting in the wings!

FOURTEEN

....

EARTHLY ANGELS AMONG US

The veil between the worlds was very thin in the weeks following Wade's death.

I awoke the morning after he passed and, with the help of my family, gathered the kids. My brother drove us back home. I was still in shock. Shortly after arriving home, I heard that there was someone at the door for me. I was just getting ready for a quick shower and figured that they would just come back and certainly not wait. But he did. He waited. I made my way downstairs to find our sweet neighbor, a seventeen-year-old old boy, waiting for me. He didn't say anything. He just looked at me. The look in his eyes was that of a servant of God. His eyes were filled with compassion and kindness. It was if our spirits connected.

In that communication, I understood that he had a deep understanding of the nature and power of God. He had had an experience that changed his perspective. To this day, I do not know what that was. Without words, I understood what he was saying, and so I just replied, "It's gonna be OK, right?"

"Yes," he said.

To understand how and why a teenage boy would come to visit me, a new widow, to bring comfort, baffled me. Most people will stay away for a while—as if a mourning person is a delicate flower they don't want to trample on. Not knowing what to do or say, many people are afraid to try to talk or visit with someone who has just suffered a catastrophic loss.

It was shown to me that this teenager was a servant of God. His visit was a tender mercy from God for me. The feeling that I experienced looking in his eyes sustained me for many months. Because of it, I knew that God knew me and was aware of my pain. He also was aware of each of my kids. He knew us. And he would continue to send angels to us!

During the first five days of mourning, I swore that I could not go on. In fact, I deliberately chose not to eat or drink. I didn't want to walk this road again. I knew the pain. Food tasted foreign. I lost my desire for hydration. Unlike previous attempts at fasting, fasting was easy now because I didn't want to feel grounded in my body anymore. I wanted just to fade away. I felt burdened by the weight of something I could not bear. It was as if dwelling less in the physical realm relieved some of the pain, and I wanted to escape.

When the flowers began arriving, I loathed them. I smelled the familiar smells of deep grief. The aroma of the condolence bouquets brought me back to the events surrounding Shay's suicide. The flowers were beautiful but still . . . I didn't want them in my house . . . again.

Meals and visitors began to arrive. One after the other. People came and went in a swirl. Everything seemed to move so fast. I had to make choices for the funeral, and yet I didn't have the strength to answer all the questions I was asked regarding the funeral and burial. This was not how my life should be! This was not my choice!

In a super short time, all the preparations were made for the day. A solid wooden casket would hold Wade's body. Red and white would be the colors of his flowers. Balloons would be released at the cemetery. Speakers were lined up. The word was spread to the communities that knew him.

Walking ten steps took effort, and all the energy I had. *God, I can't do this*, I thought. *I refuse to walk this road. I know that path. After all the meals and flowers that come, during this first little bit, the world will go silent. People will forget about me. I am the one that picks up the pieces with my kids. I know this path, and I cannot walk it. I saw my daughter walking this path. Only this time, it will be different. I will be experiencing grief not only for myself but also for my children. The thought of that is just too much to bear!*

I will be alone in my suffering with the memories of my marriage burned into my soul. Painful moments mixed with the good times, the talk of days ahead and plans for the future. Wade had talked about our future dreams most nights after the kids were tucked in bed. We looked forward to grandkids. We had good times! How can this even be happening?

I felt like an observer in a nightmare, and that nightmare was mine.

During this span, people would ask me how I was doing. I spent so many hours crying, so I remember when a couple of visitors come to my door bearing a plate of cookies. I smiled and thanked them for their thoughtfulness. I was making small talk when they mentioned, with a look both of concern and relief on their faces, that I seemed to be doing "better." I was taken aback by that. I felt frustration and was utterly annoyed!

But I learned two very important lessons at that moment. These people meant well, and they cared. They were doing the best they knew how, yet it was evident that they had never gone through what I had. They hadn't ever walked in my shoes!

Frankly, it wasn't my job to make anyone feel relieved about how I was doing! Well-intentioned people worry so much when someone is suffering that they look for any sign that that person they worry for is somehow doing better so that they can relax and not worry! They aren't sure what to do! But even so, the grief-struck person's job is *not* to make others feel better by saying the right things.

Things just are what they are. There is no right or wrong way to feel when you've suffered a loss. Each day and even minute are different. To have expectations can fill your soul with guilt, which can become the source of additional suffering.

Grief sucks. There is no way around it. There are anger and lots of tears. How was I even supposed to respond to remarks like "You seem to be doing better"? Quite literally, in that moment I was just sick of crying!

Just as I had for Brianna when she lost Shay, my sweet mom began buying me things. She felt so helpless and wanted so desperately to help me feel better. I understood her pain perfectly because I had walked in her shoes just a few months earlier. She sat with me most days. She cried with me. My extended family surrounded the kids and me during the early days. Our home was filled with visitors bringing food and flowers because people genuinely wanted to help.

I rested my head on my arms, sitting at the kitchen island. In a moment, I felt the presence of angels surrounding me. Strangely, I began to smell the aroma of a turkey dinner, a feast. It was as if they were trying to entice me to eat! I also felt Wade next to me. I began to cry and kept repeating, "I don't want food, Wade!" Stop it right now!" As I did, the aroma faded away.

I was shutting down. Deep grief was changing every cell in my body. A friend was worried I would die of a broken heart. I was never a depressed person before then. However, I now wanted to go. I knew this road. I had watched my daughter suffer in complete helplessness! To anyone who would listen, I kept saying, "The first two weeks everyone comes and visits, brings meals, but then it stops. And it should! People have their own lives to live!" Despite knowing what was to come, I was afraid of the time of being alone. I dreaded the prospect of embracing the "life goes on" attitude.

How could this state of aloneness be the rest of my life? I couldn't accept it.

I knew that I was at a crossroads. Living would come down to a choice. A simple choice, though not an easy one. Walking just a few steps took all the effort I had. I wanted to escape. Everyone said I was strong. But what if I didn't want to be "strong"?

My friend Rachelle was my angel on this side of the veil. She spent the first few nights lying beside me on a mattress next to my bed. As I was lying in my bed one evening, she walked into my room, sat next to me, and asked, "Laura, do you choose light?" I opened my swollen eyes and replied, "Yes." I knew that I didn't want darkness! I sought after light!

I needed to be carried. I believed in God. I felt him carry me so much. I also felt angels around me, lifting me. Hearing my answer, Rachelle reminded me that I needed to stay in my body, and that meant I needed to take care of it.

She then put a piece of fruit in my mouth. It felt very foreign in my mouth, having not eaten for a few days. I didn't want that fruit, but I knew I needed it. I had just chosen it.

Rachelle told me, "This is light. Water is also light," and then she gave me a drink.

That was the moment I genuinely decided I would stay. I would walk the road. I would show up fully for my kids.

I chose the light.

FIFTEEN

....

ONLY HIS SHELL

I brought my kids to the mortuary the day before the funeral so that they would be prepared in privacy to see the casket. At the last minute, I decided against my two younger children coming. My mom, dad, and brother, Aaron, joined me and my four oldest daughters. Aaron drove us in my large Suburban Wagon. The drive took an hour. The whole way I felt sick to my stomach in anticipation of seeing Wade's lifeless body.

We arrived. The mortician was not in the least bit kind. He halfheartedly mentioned that the body was in the next room rather than welcoming us in. He then joked about not spelling our names correctly on the program we would use the next day for the funeral. His behavior so annoyed me that it propelled me to ask him, "Do you believe in God?"

He said he did. But I found his behavior very odd. It seemed like he lacked compassion for our grieving family. It was if he was adding salt to an open wound.

Feeling physically weak, we decided that we would all go in together to support each other, that afterward if we wanted, we each could have a moment individually to be with him and say what we needed to say or do what we needed to do. Then we walked into the room. What I saw that day would scar my children and cause them unnecessary pain. Although the way he left this earth did not require a closed casket, Wade's body was not properly prepared for us to view it.

It is very difficult for me to write this even a few years later. I am so grateful that Spirit told me not to bring my younger kids. Wade lay on the table unclothed except for a simple white sheet covering his lifeless body. He did not have makeup on to cover the skin on his face, and he was very discolored. His skin was a blue-gray color.

I could not believe this was even real! I approached his body. I wept and cried out. I immediately laid my head on his chest. It was so surreal. I felt numb and in shock. We all gathered around. I saw my kids cautiously reaching out to touch him as I did.

I always loved Wade's hugs. He was a large man, six-three and stocky. My greatest fear had always been that one day I would lose him, and it had come true. His chest now felt cold and hard, not soft or warm like the chest of the Wade I had known.

The table his body laid on looked crude. It was narrow and worn out. In complete horror, I noticed that his arms were dangling off this table. I immediately brought both of his arms up and cradled them on his chest. I asked the mortician, "Why are his arms hanging off the table?" He very callously replied, "He is a big man."

I exclaimed, "Well, can you not get a bigger table? Can he not have dignity with his body?" He replied that the table was all he had.

Wade's head rested on a crude Styrofoam block, and the signs of an autopsy on the back of his skull were very visible. There was no dignity. This moment was one of the most difficult I have ever had to bear. To this day, it haunts me. Whenever I find myself fixated on this moment, I am softly reminded that the body is just a shell. His spirit was no longer in his body.

As I spent my alone time with Wade's body, I could only focus on his hands and hold them. His hands looked like him. His hands were large and strong. I held his hands and repeated over and over, "I'm so sorry, I'm so sorry." I softly touched his hair. As a child, he'd had thick, curly, dark brown hair. In his forties now, he was very thin on top.

I felt the coldness of his shell, and I truly felt that his suicide was my fault. I believed I caused it because he felt rejected by me. He had been struggling with his demons, and I couldn't save him anymore. But the truth is, I never could.

Until I met with our marriage counselor two weeks after his passing, I felt terrible and debilitating guilt. After she assured me his choice was not my fault, she pointed out that all I had done was hold healthy boundaries. Finally. In my heart, I could see that he didn't intend to leave this earth. He only wanted me back. He wanted me to come and save him. He wanted attention. He had done this because he struggled with mental illness and didn't know a better way to interact with me.

My brother dressed Wade in the mortuary. He was to be buried in white ceremonial clothing. This was a sacred moment. As he dressed Wade, Aaron was struck by the significance of that white clothing, and he could sense the power of the covenants we make with God.

I lay on the floor in the front entryway of the mortuary while we waited for Aaron to complete his assignment. There was a square table with tall chairs there. My girls sat around the table conversing and weeping. I also recall my parents pacing around and comforting them. The room was quite small, with a large front window that opened out to a busy main road. We had no sense of privacy or dignity.

I was lying on the floor not only because there were not enough chairs to seat us all, but because I didn't have the strength to sit up. As I closed my eyes, I could feel someone holding my hand. It was tangible. But there was no one there. I allowed myself to take comfort from whoever was holding my hand on the other side of the veil.

Each of my kids had their alone moments with their dad. From the other room, I could hear Wade's favorite songs being played on their smartphones. He loved Led Zeppelin and Leonard Skinner. They had found his playlist and saved it.

SIXTEEN

···

THE FUNERAL

One of the stages of grief is bargaining with God. For me, the bargaining internally sounded like: *Somehow, if the weather is bad and the roads are not travelable, the service won't happen. If the service doesn't happen, maybe he wasn't gone after all?* Such illogical thoughts crossed my mind. But the day came, nonetheless.

I began going through my closet. *What should I wear?* As my fingers softly touched each of my dresses, I remembered Wade telling me that my black dress with a slight sparkle was his favorite. I fondly remembered the day I wore this special dress during a recognition event for reaching a top rank in our network marketing business a few years earlier. I recalled the lively dance we did while we walked the red carpet in front of thousands of people cheering us on. The song we chose was "Thunderstruck" by ACDC. Arm in arm we did circles around each other.

That made my mind up. I would wear this dress.

After I was dressed, I explained to Brianna that this dress was her dad's favorite dress. At that moment, as clear as day, I heard Wade say, "It still is."

It felt as if we were all getting ready for church. I could feel his presence as if he were with me. This is partly what made seeing his lifeless body seem surreal. I dressed Wes in his favorite church shirt. His dad had a similar one, and on Sundays, they would dress to match. My son had loved that they matched. I combed his soft, blond hair and kissed his chubby cheeks. He would look so handsome that day.

Laura, keep your shoulders up, I kept telling myself. *Breathe.*

We made our way to the church. It was a short drive as the church was only a mile away. It was a warm summer morning. My stomach ached.

As if to add to the pain of it all, the hearse carrying Wade's body was late to arrive. When it got there, the driver opened the door, and some trash fell out of the front seat. The driver, who was wearing a much too tight shirt, stood there casually sipping a Big Gulp. I was mortified.

We waited as Wade's body was brought into a private viewing room. His mom went in alone and very quickly came out. She was visibly torn up and said, "Don't go in there." My heart sunk. Was his body still not prepared? I made my way into the room. I saw him. Dressed in his white clothing. My heart broke for his mom. She saw her only son. Lifeless. His body was prepared.

To see my husband of twenty-two years laying lifeless in the casket was too much to bear. I do believe that in between the complete meltdowns I was having my body was going into denial. The scene didn't feel real. For one thing, I could *feel* Wade with us. I would talk to him, and yet his body was cold and firm. Lifeless. We would not hear his deep voice again.

It was terrible to watch my kids cry over their father. One at a time, they went into the viewing room to be with their dad alone and say goodbye. I decided not to allow my son to see him at all, as he might find it upsetting. When the kids were done paying their respects, the rest of the family and a few close friends were allowed in.

A chair was placed next to the coffin for me. I rested my head on the edge of the coffin and took Wade's hand in mine. Those moments are difficult to put into words. My stomach ached. It felt as if I was watching myself from a distance.

My brother-in-law left the viewing room and went into the chapel where the service would be held long before any guests arrived. He later related to me that he was struck by experiencing the presence of angels. When my niece joined him in the chapel a few minutes later, she felt the same presence.

While still in the viewing room, we had a family prayer. Wade's sacred temple clothing was placed symbolically on him. Final photos were taken of Wade. Our children gathered together around the casket as one final family photo was taken.

The casket was closed. As a family, we followed the casket into the chapel and found our seats. As I walked down the aisle, I saw so many familiar faces from the life we shared together.

The service to honor Wade's life was extraordinarily long. I sat in the front row next to our little son. My daughters filled the rest of the same church pew. Our immediate family sat in the first couple of pews behind us. Many memories were shared from the dais. His best friend from childhood, Jason, spoke of Wade as a youth and of his struggles at the end of his life.

Here is a transcript of Jason's remarks.

I am a Wade expert. We've been compadres for forty-four years (since age two). His family moved next door to mine in 1972, and we remained next-door neighbors for the next seventeen years until we both left on missions. During those early years, we spent countless hours together. We did all the usual stupid things kids do, among them breaking windows, building forts in the yard, climbing on the roof and jumping off, getting stung by hornets, crashing our bikes after designing elaborate ramps that were far too high, with compact gravel as our landing site.

By the way, we never used bike helmets back in the 1970s and 1980s. Heck, even seatbelts were optional.

We shot each other with BB guns, climbed cliffs, jumped off cliffs onto rockslides below or into murky river water, whatever the case may have been. We learned how to drive and did so very poorly. Usually with a stereo that could be heard for several blocks. We nearly blew off each other's hands with M80s. Set up pranks for passing vehicles, which involved people-shaped dummies lying in the middle of the road attached to fishing line.

I'm not making this stuff up. Somehow, we survived and moved on to become young adults. Both of our dads taught us the value of work, so we did have that going for us.

We eventually both somehow convinced very beautiful women to marry us, despite both of us being plagued with unsightly curly hair that was a common style back in 1994. As kids and family became a front priority, we drifted apart somewhat for some time. But these past several months, we've been closer than ever and have had many deep conversations about life, relationships, and our own struggles with the love of self. We had long talks about being good husbands and fathers. He was anxiously trying to improve himself all the way to the very end.

One of Wade's gifts was his incomparable sense of humor. It permeated everything he did. I remember he used to distort his face into all kinds of characters. To where he was totally unrecognizable. I would laugh so hard that I could hardly breathe. He was always putting on a little comedy show. If you spent enough time around Wade, you know, he was a walking repertoire of impressions and voices, which he would activate in any ordinary setting.

He wasn't doing this stuff to please a crowd either. He would jump into character roles, often when it was just me and him or a couple of family members.

This was before political correctness. His repertoire of stereotypes included an English-speaking Mexican guy with a heavy accent, a high-pitched and animated Chinese guy, a gay guy with a heavy lisp (no offense), and several different classes of British guys. And then there was his impression of Julia Childs, the TV personality and chef.

He was also a man of a thousand sound effects. If you have ever watched Bugs Bunny and Friends on a Saturday morning, you know there are a lot of things going on in the background as the characters play out different scenes. A lot of sounds are happening. Like jumping sounds, or the sound of someone getting smacked upside the head. I don't know when this started, but Wade became a master at the art of making these little sounds and would constantly weave them into everyday life. I remember him narrating a scene once when there were some deer that had gotten into the yard, and as they bounded away, hurdling the fence, he would add "Pawr, pawr, pawr!" Just to give more depth and comedy to the situation at hand. It was always going on: nunchucks, swords, ninja fights, or someone running off "chekchekchekah!" It was always fun to just hang out with Wade because there was always laughter. It occurred to me just recently that he got a lot of that from his dad, Larry. Larry was the original sound and character orchestrator.

Somewhere along the line, Wade came up with a pet name for himself: Sir Lawrence Waderick Reginald

Esquire, III. He would use that to refer to himself on occasion, always with a heavy British accent. He loved Monty Python movies. Usually, when he got into this mode, he would keep it going with, "Jeeves, bring the car around and, pardon me, but do you have any Gray Poupon?"

Everyone knows Wade was a large guy. At six-foot-three-inches and 250 pounds, even in his younger days, he was physically strong but gentle. I've heard others refer to him as a teddy bear and I think that description fits.

Wade was generous and kindhearted and was service-oriented. He often put his physical strength to good use and would be engaged in service projects, like helping people move, doing yardwork, or hoisting engine blocks and pianos. He had ambitions early in his professional career to reach out to troubled individuals, in particular, youth, to try and lift them to a better place. He pursued his education in professional counseling and earned a master's degree in psychology. Even this last week, when we spoke on the phone, he was putting together his resume to start working again at the local youth center. He knew he wouldn't make a lot of money at the job, but he felt it was something he could do that might help give him a feeling purpose, which he was seeking lately. He cared about others. I think his gentle teddy-bear persona was especially calming to those that he worked with at a local drug and alcohol treatment facility. He had a natural instinct for listening to others and helping them solve their personal problems.

In recent years, he had shifted his focus to building a family business with Laura and evolved into a successful businessman and motivator, working alongside her. Somewhere in the journey, he started coming up with his now-famous "Wade-isms." They were essentially the world according to Wade on various topics. Sage advice he would give out unsolicited. Many people followed him on various social networks.

He was a complete man, a valued, loved human being, a husband, a father, a brother, a son, a leader, and a friend. He was loved by many.

I need to shift gears a bit. I want to talk to Wade's children: Brianna, Caitlyn, Alyssa, Emma, Grace, and little Wes. I call you out individually because I know that he cared about each one of you. He treasured you. Your father was one of the most decent men of character that I have known. We shared a mutual respect for one another. I want to emphasize this truth that he always loved you, will continue to love you, and will never stop. Do not doubt yourselves. He will continue to support you from the other side. He had an illness. His mind was *afflicted. He did NOT abandon you. This thing that happened is not your fault. Please don't ever think that you are not enough because your father is not here physically. He is here in spirit. He continues on, and I will assure you now of this truth: He will be watching over you. You can have conversations with him. He will comfort you. He is at peace now.*

We don't fully understand depression. Just like cancer, it affects people in different ways and to varying degrees. It is a disease that affects the physiology of the brain. We know that Wade was struggling to cope with and fight severe health issues over several years. We really don't know what was happening for Wade and we weren't there during his final moments. But we cannot judge him, or anyone else for that matter. Those moments don't define him, nor are they representative of his life. Let God sort that out. It is his alone to sort out. I was with Wade constantly growing up. You'll just have to trust me. There were plenty of times when we both should have died from multiple causes. He was permitted to live on and become a husband and father, a provider, a counselor, a businessman, a friend. He played many roles during his rich life. We were blessed to have him in our lives and feel of his warmth, his laughter, his kindness, and all else that he was.

I shall acknowledge here the herculean efforts of Laura, his lovely wife. She carried a heavy load for many years, being his life partner as they both struggled against the effects of his depression. What can we say other than that she is an amazing person of strength and character? Unquestionably, Wade loved Laura more than anyone else in this world. Her gifts of kindness, patience, and willingness to be the supportive spouse over many years were the perfect complement to his life struggles.

I want to talk a little bit about God. I believe that God knows us each individually. What is the common theme we hear anytime someone passed but then comes back? There are many accounts of this documented. Some have written stories about it. All are very similar.

A burden is lifted. The person feels no shame. There is a feeling of total acceptance and love. Almost always, the person who has passed does not want to come back to this mortal life.

I believe that type of experience is a glimpse into the true nature of God and how he feels about each one of us as his children.

That is a pattern we see as we read the scriptures and learn of charity, the pure love of Christ. It is to be patient, kind, filled with empathy toward other people, and gentle. As a general rule, we are too hard on ourselves and especially in the church, for some reason. But it doesn't need to be that way. I don't believe that is God's way. He has taught us a different path.

The Atonement that Christ made for humankind is about us being able to gain forgiveness and recover from our mistakes. Jesus suffered for our sins. However, the Atonement he made was also an ongoing gift to us to relieve ALL our suffering. We can rely on him at this time when we are feeling so low, so empty, and so discouraged. When we're coping with our loss. There is strength available to all of us as we seek him in prayer and ask for his support. When we cannot make sense of the "why" behind different circumstances in our lives, it is OK just to give it over to the Lord. Let him carry the burden for you. It's OK to say, "I don't understand all of this, and I can't make sense of it right now. I'm going to let this go." As Christ is our elder and wiser brother who went before us, we CAN rely on HIM.

Pain and suffering are inevitable. They are part of our earthly experience. How often do we seek distraction from personal pain? Powerful distractions in all forms, among them addictions to substances and processes, like viewing pornography, consuming drugs and alcohol, playing video games, spending excessive time doing social networking online. There are workaholics, shopaholics, sex addicts, and the list goes on. We can even turn to other people as an addiction. This is codependence.

These are all forms of self-slavery. These pursuits might alter the mind for a time and give us a temporary feeling of comfort. However, they are hollow and lead to personal destruction if left unchecked. Let us learn to trust God and turn to him. We are all valuable in the sight of God. We are all his children, and he loves us. It is in him and through him that we will come to realize our own strength and worth as human beings.

There may be those in this congregation who are feeling levels of guilt for events or things that happened or didn't, like not saying things that could have been said; or you may be wondering if something could have been done differently so that the outcome would have been different. Please don't do that. This is sad and very hard, but let those feelings go. Wade is at peace now. I felt that from him directly. Move forward with peace in your heart. That is what he would have wanted for us. That is what the Lord wants us to do!

Our dear family friend Jen sang the most beautiful rendition of "I Know My Redeemer Lives." The congregation was completely silent, and I dare say that there was not a dry eye as we listened to and felt this comforting hymn. Jen later recounted to me that she strongly felt the spirit of the Lord and a heavenly presence next to her as she sang.

There was no doubt to anyone in that chapel that the room was, indeed, filled with a heavenly host! At one point, as Jen was singing, her voice cracked. It was then that she felt a presence move behind her she later told me.

Jen had been Wade's voice coach. She had been helping him prepare for a concert in which he was to sing "Halleluiah," a song about the biblical story of David. He was so proud that he would be performing, and I could remember him practicing the song in our home prior to our separation. His voice was deep, and he sang with emotion. He had always wanted to be good enough to sing in church with our daughters at a sacrament meeting. This was on his bucket list, as he would say.

At the funeral, Jen truly sang for Wade and became his voice. She knew of his love for the Savior. I will never forget those moments when the spirit of the Lord in the room was so strong. To feel complete and desperate sorrow and complete and utter peace, joy, and love simultaneously is an experience that is etched into my soul.

The church halls were crowded as we made our way outside once the service ended. I found myself surrounded by friends and family from all phases and areas of my life. I was surprised at seeing some of the far-flung friends who had made it a point not to miss this remembrance.

One such friend approached me in a manner unlike anyone else's. She first gave me a very big hug and then pulled away and held me firmly by my shoulders. She then spoke plainly to me, and her words clearly held power. "This is for a purpose, and you are going to be OK." There was no lightly tiptoeing around the issue at hand with her. She was there to give me the spiritual gift that I needed at that moment. She lent me her strength.

I will always remember the feeling I had at that moment. It was then that I truly recognized everyone has unique God-given gifts.

A very bizarre windstorm picked up as everybody stood outside of the church building. It came out of nowhere. I heard comments that we were wanted at the cemetery and to hurry into our cars and get there, implying that the windstorm had been spiritually created to get us moving faster. I later learned that many people had already arrived at the cemetery, and my dad, who was dedicating the grave, was unaware that I wasn't there yet. He was about to say the dedication prayer when my brother stopped him to inform him to wait for me. I still have thoughts about the random, very strong wind that hit us at that exact moment.

Following the dedication prayer, my sister-in-law arranged for us to release a bouquet of red, white, and blue balloons as a symbol to honor Wade and release the pain of losing him. The colors were emblems of the U.S. flag. Wade loved and was deeply loyal to the United States of America. He always kept up to date on political events and was knowledgeable about the nation's history.

The weather was warm. I welcomed the brightness of the sun. After the dedication prayer, I took off my shoes and lay barefooted in the grass next to the burial place of Wade and also Shay. I was wearing a small silver bracelet with a little charm that had small wings on it. I looked down to find that the little wings had fallen off between the prayer and the release of the balloons. Seeing this, I was struck with the insight that all things come from God and will return to him one day. It may sound strange, but I was searching for meaning in every small thing I saw. As I did this, many more spiritual messages began to show up and reveal truths for me.

SEVENTEEN

···

TENDER MERCIES

At the time of Wade's passing, many people reached out to me and told me what a difference he had made in their lives. Someone said that because of Wade, she had achieved success in her business. A lonely older man in our neighborhood who had recently lost his beloved wife of many years described how Wade was so concerned for his welfare that he just showed up with our older girls to help him. Wade had gathered rags and cleaners. Then he knocked on the man's door and announced that they were there to clean his house.

In addition, several people shared with me what they had seen Wade's spiritual body during our period of mourning. A young family member told me she saw Wade dressed in white and standing next to me with his hand resting on my shoulder as if to comfort me.

I still felt as if I could text or call him regarding concerns with our kids. Rather than talking to him face to face, I found myself closing my eyes and communicating without words. At one point while in my bedroom alone, I played a favorite song (Alan Jackson's "Remember When") and held my arms out as if he were there dancing with me. Tears flowed freely on a regular basis. I felt as if my spirit communicated with his, perfectly. The feelings of anger would later surface as I began to heal.

I am forever grateful for the spiritual messengers living on this side of the veil. The comfort I received from another dear friend several weeks after the funeral was immense. He shared the following account with me.

As the funeral started and the first speaker spoke, I experienced emotions similar to those of the stories and sentiments expressed. When the second speaker began speaking, the Holy Ghost prompted me to stop responding emotionally to the words and instead to focus on their spiritual essence. I obeyed the prompting. Immediately, I saw Wade standing next to the casket directly in front of you and your daughter Caitlyn. He was dressed in white and appeared tall and trim with broad shoulders. His spiritual body appeared to be in his mid-twenties, but his countenance appeared to have the wisdom of eternity. He only conveyed one emotion: 100 percent of his intent and focus was on being there to comfort those who attended. His eyes were intently watching you and your family with the goal of relieving your pain and suffering in every instant and in every way.

As Wade prayed, I recognized that he was praying on behalf of different individuals, naming them by name as he prayed. There was no judgment or sorrow, only an overwhelming desire to comfort each beloved family member, friend, and stranger in the room.

The service went long (as you know), but I was filled with the Spirit and so enjoyed watching Wade work and pray for you and your children and others in the congregation that I didn't want it to end. As people around me began checking their watches or the text messages on their phones and eventually stepping out quietly, I was enthralled to feel what I felt and witness what I witnessed. I am so grateful that the meeting lasted as long as it did, and I could have easily spent many more hours watching what was happening.

Wade didn't appear calm or serene. Instead, he was focused. I want to say that he was intense, but it is more appropriate to say he was intently working. His focus flashed between you and literally everyone else who was there individually. For every time his eyes darted towards someone else, they darted right back to you, then across the front row, back to you, and then back to others in the congregation.

I can't say enough how focused and how quick he was. His eyes would fix on someone, and then he would close his eyes and plead for them by their first and last name. I didn't recognize many of the names, but my heart leaped when he said Michelle, mostly because I recognized her name, but also because of how intently he prayed that she would understand the gift of the Holy Ghost. I turned around and looked, and sure enough, she was there, which surprised me, and I also saw that she appeared visibly shaken.

I found it interesting that Wade didn't pray as much for your young son as he did for your other children, but I did notice that when he looked at him, he beamed with love and joy. I've thought about this quite a bit, and I believe it's because, your son appeared to be OK during the funeral—mostly just restless like any preschooler would be.

There were many names that I didn't recognize, and that I don't remember, but yours was repeated over and over, Laura. I heard him pray that you and the children and his parents would forgive him. This was like 1/1000th *of his praying, however, because the other 999/1000th of the time he was praying for each person to be comforted.*

I was also surprised that he said, "In Jesus' name" and "In the name of Jesus," in his prayers. I never heard him pray during his life, but it seemed different from the nomenclature I'm used to in church where everyone ends their prayers "In the name of Jesus Christ, amen." It seemed more personal—like he knew him and was invoking the name of a friend or a brother, not a distant authority figure.

I can bear testimony that Wade's stewardship of you and the children is still in full and complete effect. He has much work to do, for sure (those spirits, they're always rushing about), but he is and will be taking every opportunity he can to watch you, to pray on your behalf, to whisper to you, and to influence all things for your good.

I can't imagine the pain and distance you're experiencing, but I can add my testimony to that all of those who have testified: He is here and will continue to be. His absence will hurt, but it will only hurt as much as is for your good. Comfort will come.

Thank you so much for being in tune and receptive enough to receive this. I don't intend to portray that I received any revelation for you, only to share what was given for me in the hope that it may also be of comfort and service to you.

I feel like I can share two last things with you. First, there was the spirit of a woman standing beside Wade. She was primarily interested in your son. She was much smaller than Wade, petite. She wore a long white dress, and I would describe her as fair-looking with a kind face. I didn't hear her say anything.

Second, I feel the reason I saw what I saw has to do with my own search and hope for understanding. I have suffered from minor depression and anxiety, and I think this helped me form a kinship with Wade. Seeing what I saw was another testament of the eternal nature of our Father's plan and helped me to better understand how brilliant the spirit is when it is unfettered from the mortal body. I also got a peek at the glory that will come when the spirit is reunited with an immortal body. I'm so grateful for the mercy of the Atonement and our all-knowing father's plan.

How I wished I could have seen Wade in spirit myself. *Why couldn't I have the spiritual gift of clairvoyance?* I wondered. I longed to "see" something! I bargained with God. *I will do anything you ask only to have one last visit with him.*

Those tender mercies were preparing me for what was to come.

....

EIGHTEEN

MY VISION OPENS

To some the gift of visions is given. To others, the gift to feel or to hear. While I was mourning Wade's departure, my suffering was so great that much of the time I felt in between worlds. Little glimpses of beauty became visible to my physical eye. I began to notice and feel things, not of this world. Symbols began appearing everywhere, proving the existence of the other side to me. It was real.

During the months following Wade's death, it was a regular occurrence for me to see angelic orbs of light, something I had never seen before! One night, in particular, the veil between worlds was very thin. I was deep in prayer, "Father, help me. Bring me courage and strength," when I felt a sensation of comfort that was not of this world. I began to see orbs of light all around my bed. In a fast *whoosh,* a blueish purple streak of light flashed by me that was approximately three feet long. The best way to describe the light is that it was the most brilliant color, and it was alive.

There was no doubt that I was not alone. I felt comfort and peace. My physical body was warm and comforted. I had always had many fears, one being to lose someone close to me. I had imagined grief would feel terrible, lonely, and suffocating. And yet, here I was living through it and experiencing complete and utter calm due to the tender mercies that had been shared with me. I knew that I had help on the other side. The spirits were very concerned about me. They stayed with me.

One of my greatest fears after Wade's passing was that I would be forgotten after the funeral. I didn't necessarily want more brownies or cookies from kind neighbors, but I also could not imagine just going about life as usual. The routine sounded like an impossible task. When I went to that place of fear, I felt panicky. But in very dark moments, I would feel the presence of angels surrounding me. They were tangible. From time to time, I would feel the gentle pressure of a hand on my shoulder or hear whispers messages of comfort. Signs were continually presented to me. I prayed and believed. I sought for heavenly assistance in every moment of every day. And soon it became very clear to me that I did not need to be afraid for I would never be alone.

I was so curious as to who the guardian angel of my son was that Wade's friend had seen during the funeral. Searching through photos of our ancestors and presenting them to this friend, he confirmed that without a doubt the petite woman he saw watching over my Wes was Wade's great-grandmother.

Tears flowed continually from my eyes during this tender time. My testimony grew. I knew without a doubt that the "feelings" I would receive randomly were not so random! The veil was so thin. And we are all connected! Our ancestors are still very much involved in our lives. Why would they not be? We are a family!

My vision was opening.

NINETEEN

···

A BLESSING FROM HEAVEN

My home was abuzz for several weeks with friends dropping off endless amounts of cookies and condolences. I rested in my recliner in the main living room. This room was quite large, with vaulted ceilings. The previous owner of our house was an artist. His art studio had been remodeled into this living space, which we called the *great room.* The floors were light wood with custom-built, dark wood cabinets throughout the room. It was furnished with several leather couches as well as the recliner.

Alone in the great room, I could hear the many conversations of visitors in the kitchen, which was divided from where I sat by white French doors.

One afternoon, a couple of days after the funeral, I closed my eyes and let my tears run down my cheeks. Suddenly a feeling of peace and comfort washed over me. I began to feel the slight pressure of hands resting softly on my head. There were at least two pairs of hands. I was so astonished by this sensation that I opened my eyes to see who had joined me from the kitchen, but I could not see anyone with my physical eyes.

I was filled with so much warmth and joy that my tears quickly became tears of gratitude. Gratitude that I was not alone. The hands from the other side of the veil remained on my head for roughly fifteen minutes, during which time I recognized that I was being administered to.

This experience was so precious to me that I didn't tell anyone about it for quite a while. I held it sacred and recognized it as a tender mercy that I would forever cherish.

When the invisible hands were no longer touching me, the thought then came to my mind: *Don't let this go to waste.* It was a spiritual "download."

I would receive similar spiritual downloads throughout the first few weeks, some so intensely flooding my senses that at times, I felt as if I was living in two different worlds. The feeling would be accompanied by very specific instruction and intent. *Testify of me, and you will heal.*

I would acknowledge that feeling and nod my head and sometimes say out loud, "Thank you." I recognized it as a message from God.

Praying became like drinking the most delicious cold water on a hot summer day. I thirsted for God's comfort! I spent many hours on my knees in my closet. It was the most private place I could pray given I had a house full of kids. It was a small walk-in closet with racks on either side. A small row of hooks held a variety of necklaces. Hanging from one particularly long chain were our wedding rings. I wore this necklace with our rings during the funeral. We had chosen our rings at a local mall twenty-two years earlier, two months before we were to be married. Physically I was "alone," but in those moments down on my knees on the purple carpet in my closet, I did not feel in the least bit alone. My prayers were heard. I felt comfort that was not of this world.

I received several blessings from kindhearted people in the weeks to come. I can recall one that reaffirmed the message not to let my pain go to waste. During another, I was told that if I turned to the Savior, he would give me strength of body, mind, and spirit. The very kind man who administered this particular blessing told me that the blessing that would always be answered immediately, to those that ask for it is a blessing for strength.

During yet another blessing, I was told: "Do not let this experience be for naught."

There it was. Another tender mercy.

I was receiving direct messages from our loving Father in heaven continuously because I was praying so much every day. And I often spent time in my car alone in prayer because my prayers were not the quiet, whispering type. Two weeks after Wade passed, I was deep in prayer sitting in the Suburban out in the driveway. In desperation and pain, I screamed to my Father in heaven. "Guide me, comfort me, comfort my children, send angels to each of them. Please surround us with heavenly help."

In response, in my head I heard: *You will be married in one year and your life will be much different than it is today.*

I opened my eyes and went, *What?!?!* I felt comfort not of this world. My tears dried while I pondered that download.

And the next thought that came to me, as clear as the rising sun, was that part of Wade's healing and progression on the other side was to make sure that I am loved and not alone. You see, he was still connected to me. The fact is, he will always be.

TWENTY

....

RUNNING WITH ANGELS

One of my favorite things is an early summer run. I love the sounds of the sprinklers and the smell of freshly cut grass. It is pure bliss! I have been running regularly since I was in my early teens. Even during each of my pregnancies, I would continue to exercise. Sweating has always helped me cope in trying times.

That September, a few weeks after Wade passed, I felt the nudge to go out for a run. I had decided not just to survive but to live fully again. This didn't mean I wasn't sad. Crying was now a part of my daily life. But I wanted to face every day with courage. Deep down, God knew that I was "all in."

Lacing up my shoes meant so much more than just another sweat. It meant that I was choosing strength. I would face my pain, and I would run, even with the pain.

I would run through the pain or walk the road, if that was all I could do, until the next time when it would be a little bit easier.

This would be my first run since the date of Wade's passing. When someone dies, people begin to refer to events around that time as happening before or after it. This is because a severe loss is a trauma that changes your life. It is as if you have moved to a different planet!

On this occasion, I felt pretty good. I put on my running shoes and tied my hair back in a ponytail. I put on some good tunes—I believe it was a full album of Led Zeppelin, and then I left the house and ran. I ran through the pain. With every step, I felt a release.

I was approaching Main Street, which is a stretch of about two miles when I began to pick up my pace. As I did this, I sensed the presence of many angels running both alongside and behind me. It was as if I had legions of angels quite literally propelling me forward.

My run that day was effortless. I wasn't tired because I was being carried. That was the feeling.

Subsequent runs were not as easy, and I tried to recreate this tender mercy, tried to feel close to what I felt that day—as supported—but I couldn't feel it.

It didn't matter though. What I had experienced that day bolstered me emotionally for several months. It was another reminder that I was not alone.

TWENTY-ONE

....

WHEN THE MOMENTS
HIT IN PUBLIC

Deeply grieving is like entering a different world. Nothing is as it once was.

How I ate, slept, and breathed had changed. Even my sense of smell had changed. The unfamiliarity of the ordinary felt like a challenge to my survival. Taking my first trip to the grocery shop seemed an impossible task. Walking ten steps took all my strength. It was easy for me now to grasp how someone could die from a broken heart. To go several hours without a complete breakdown somehow felt like progress.

I decided I needed to send Wade's CPAP machine, which he used for sleep apnea, to my father-in-law, so I took myself to the local post office. There was a small line ahead of me. I just needed help boxing it. The address was ready. I approached the man at the counter.

Hearing his simple question, "How can I help?" I burst into tears.

While ugly crying, I did my best to explain that I needed help to properly package the CPAP. "This was my husband's. He passed. I must get this to his dad. I needed tape. I need a box. And I can't find a box!" He looked at me with sympathy and kindness, and he helped me, while another worker had just looked on as I sobbed.

I had no idea that one human's eyes could produce so many tears!

At moments like this one, I felt as if I were an observer of myself. *This cannot be me!* I thought. *This isn't how I planned my life.* Upon entering my car, I surrendered to the cleansing of tears.

I will never forget this kindly postal worker who helped me. It may have taken an extra five minutes for him to help me prepare the box but what a difference it made to me.

I spent many hours in my closet, crying out to my Father in heaven. Grief knocked me to my knees. My compassion grew as I developed more understanding of those in a deep state of grief.

I felt the love of so many people. For example, a dear friend and her daughter-in-law tied white ribbons on all the trees in the front yard—a beautiful gesture of remembrance. Each had a brief, simple message written on it sent from individuals I had known in my essential oils business.

Even though I was being supported and encouraged by so many people, every step was painful. I dreaded what life would be like in a few weeks after the well-wishers had shifted their focus back to their own lives. Would I and my children be forgotten?

The stages of grief do not go in any particular order. There can be no judgment placed on those that mourn deeply. There is no "getting over it." Crying doesn't mean that someone is doing "badly." Crying is part of the healing process. Anger is quite good too. But not everybody understands that it is.

Just weeks after Wade's funeral, I confided to someone that I felt angry and frustrated. "How could he leave me behind to pick up all the pieces?" I said.

This well-meaning person told me that I should not feel angry because Wade was in a "better place," and anger was "not healthy for me." But how could that be fair?

This person was not present with my children 24/7. He did not have to witness their pain. He had no idea how cruel I felt that Wade had been to leave us as he did. I was the one upon whom my children relied. I was the one that would have to make the therapy appointments, urge them to continue to attend school, and tuck them in at night by myself. I was the one who would have to be strong. Who else would do these things? Wade was gone, and now I was a single parent with six offspring, including two under the age of eight.

My son would ask me nightly to sing songs to him about his daddy. For the first few months, I cried through those songs. The songs were memories. They went something like this: "Daddy mowed the lawn with you, and you had so much fun with him," "Daddy took you to the dinosaur museum," "Daddy called you 'my son,' and he would wrestle with you." I sang to a random tune, but to my little son, the sound was comforting. I knew it was helping him process everything that was going on. But some nights I was so exhausted that I simply didn't want to do it! I was tired of trying to explain why Daddy wasn't coming home. Ever. That he was gone from this life.

Wes struggled with separation anxiety for a long time. I couldn't leave the room without him having a complete meltdown. But can you blame him? His world had been shattered. In a very short span, the two men he had known the best were ripped from his life.

TWENTY-TWO

....

MIRACLES

My focus was 100 percent on my children. We began attending therapy for trauma regularly as a family. The clinic that we attended was specific for trauma. Much of the time, I felt numb and in shock that this was my life! I felt that we didn't belong there! I was in denial. I found comfort in keeping myself busy, which fortunately was not hard to do, being a mom of six. The kids did art therapy. I was so proud of my oldest, daughter, Brianna as she chose a more positive way to deal with loss. Rather than numb the pain, she faced it. Week after week she met with her therapist (who had herself experienced severe trauma). Brianna is truly a remarkable young woman!

A couple of months after Wade passed, I sent Caitlyn and Alyssa to Guatemala for two weeks to do service. We celebrated every miracle, every ray of light. I was grasping at anything to give them a sense of purpose and to help them heal. We volunteered at the homeless shelter. They took horseback riding lessons.

I paid special attention to one of my daughters, earnestly praying for her to be OK. She had struggled in the past and been diagnosed with fibromyalgia that was brought on by stress. I prayed continually for her safety and protection. The slightest worry for her would send my heart racing and make my legs go weak. I prayed for answers and guidance. Then the windows of heaven opened, and I found her a new school to attend that specialized in performing arts. This was her passion.

My therapist told me about the school. It sounded ideal, so I called and set up an appointment the next day for a tour. My daughter was resistant at the thought of it. She wanted to be homeschooled. But I knew that homeschooling with this very creative and social child would not be in her best interest! Each of the children's needs was different. I encouraged her to come to visit it with me, suggesting that it wouldn't hurt at least to look at the school. Ultimately, she would decide if she attended or not, I told her.

The entire drive I prayed silently. I pleaded with God, "Please let her be open to this school. Help her find her place, her voice again! May the right people connect with her!" We pull into a very small parking lot. The building was red brick and ran the length of the small parking lot. It had large windows that read: Pioneer Performing Arts. We heard the familiar sound of a popular rock song being played. It sounded so good that I could barely tell that students were performing this song! They were so talented! She decided to attend that school, and it proved to be a tremendous blessing for her. She found her voice in performing arts and had a successful, fun graduation.

I needed to remind myself on a regular basis to stand upright and with my shoulders back. Something as simple as standing tall was a challenge for me. The burden of grief felt so heavy that my shoulders slumped. The sheer weight of gravity and pain were difficult to bear! It was not only emotionally hard but physically hard and painful as well. I felt as if I were carrying a load of heavy boulders on my shoulders.

My heart also hurt, and I had constant stomachaches. I was bracing myself for survival. Much of my time, I was in a *trauma response* mode. It would take me many months of reprogramming and healing to allow my shoulders to relax and for me to breathe deeply again.

I wish I could say that praying one time and asking for help was enough. It wasn't. I felt like: *Heavenly Father knows what I need. Do I have to ask every day? Can't he read my mind?* But as clear as day, every time I asked, he was there for me with assistance. He was there! I asked, and angels surrounded my home. They were as tangible to me as the people on this side of the veil that would visit me! I began to thirst for this constant spiritual companionship.

Seeking out comfort and daily direction was routine. One of my favorite places for strength was in my closet on my knees. "Father, hear me," I pleaded. I spent many hours in my closet, praying. My sister recently told me that those first weeks after he passed were some of the sweetest and most difficult times. She told me that for her, the feeling of angels in my home was tangible too. They were there! They were there because I not only asked, I pleaded. It was simply too painful to walk the road of survival alone!

Ultimately, there were minutes and hours when I felt so much peace and joy that it was as if I was being carried by angels! They truly walked with me!

TWENTY-THREE

....

THE PATH TO HEALING

In the weeks and months following Wade's death I no longer was concerned about "normal" stuff. I had lost my attachment to things and expectations of how things "should" be. How I wished I could complain about normal things again. However, I was in the refiner's fire of mourning and had entered another dimension of being.

I had never experienced a complete loss of desire for things of this world. Desire for food and water completely left me. I was making a daily decision to choose light, but still day after day, my body was shutting down. The grief was so heavy I could barely move. My eyes were beginning to look sunken in. I didn't go to the bathroom much during the day, but when I did, I noticed my urine was a color I didn't recognize—dark brown. I was dehydrated. I kept coming back to that moment a few days following Wade's passing when Rachelle reminded me that I needed to care for my body. After that, my eyes began to open. The realization that I could never leave my children entered my heart. I decided I would choose light for them. I wouldn't just survive. I would live each day fully—as if it were my last. And I prayed earnestly for strength. This would be a prayer I prayed often in the coming months, one that would always be answered.

Somehow, the sun still rose and set. The hours turned into days. Yet it was if time was standing still.

We had a warm fall. I spent a lot of time sitting on the window seat in the front room watching the leaves on our large walnut tree sway and flutter with the wind.

Certain experiences stand out to me during this time that I will hold close to my heart. I do believe that there is a lesson in this pain that I feel that the Lord is teaching me. My neighbor Holly came to me several times, bringing essential oils for healing with her. I recall in very dark hours, feeling her massage my feet with them. As she did, she whispered, "No judgment. You are loved."

I recall the woodsy aromas. I felt enveloped in safety. I was in a safe place to feel what was. I could grieve with her. She showed me Christ-like love. She mourned with me. She wasn't afraid of my tears. She gave me a priceless gift of a simple stone necklace imbued with meaning that I wear to this day as a reminder that there is light even in dark times. The stone appears dark on first glance. But when light hits it or you study it up close, light sparkles in it become visible.

I will never forget Holly's kindness. This was a pivotal point for me in my personal path to healing. My friend walked the road with me for a time. She was a busy mom, running a hair-cutting business in addition to running her household. And yet, the moments she spent with me were so tender. She didn't place expectations on what I should be feeling. She didn't even say much. She willingly shared my pain.

Another neighbor, Kim, brought me a much-needed gift: several boxes of Kleenex tissues. They were the super-soft kind. She simply showed up and handed them to me. We embraced as she told me she loved me, and then she left. Kim was the one who showed up (one-year post-death) to help me pack up my house to move to a new home. For hours on end, despite back pain, she prepared boxes, filled them, and helped me clean each room once its contents had been packed for transport.

I treasure those memories of friends being there for me and my children. We were so blessed to live near many of our immediate family members. They were there with us continually the first couple of weeks.

On Saturday mornings, I would hear the lawn being cut by a neighbor. He and his son offered to help for several months. Without pay and without any expectation, they just showed up and began to work to make my lawn beautiful. There were signs everywhere that I would be given what I needed when I needed it. To this day, when I think of my home in Mapleton, Utah, I am filled with immense gratitude. Despite the pain that occurred, angels dwelt in this home. This was the home where the Savior held my hand and carried me, a home that was so filled with the spirit of the Lord that at times, I felt my feet were not touching the floor.

....

TWENTY-FOUR

IMMORTALIZED IN
TATTOO ART

There is no greater vulnerability than that of a mourning widow or child. Big decisions should not be made soon after the loss of a spouse or parent. Thinking can be too clouded. I can see this clearly now as I look back at my choices and behavior in that very tender time.

But you can also have otherworldly experiences that are beautiful. Just a few days following Wade's passing, my adult daughters, Brianna, Caitlyn, and Alyssa, had the idea to get small tattoos on their wrists. All three chose a few words from letters that their dad had recently written to them in his own handwriting while he was staying at the hospital following his failed attempted suicide and took these to a tattoo artist for rendering in ink. They described to me the spiritual experience they had that day.

Upon walking into the tattoo parlor, they explained to the artist that their dad had just passed away. The kind man asked what music their dad liked. He then went on to play Wade's playlist of songs from Led Zeppelin to Jimmy Hendrix while he worked. His favorite music filled the shop. Tears were shed, and they reported feeling that their dad was with them without a doubt.

While I am not a tattoo lover, I recognize that there is beauty in even things that I don't understand.

TWENTY-FIVE

....

READING TO MY SON

As you may recall, my friend Rachelle stayed with us on a few tough nights following Wade's death, to help me cope. She saw everything that transpired between me and my children, including a tender time with my three-year-old son, Wes, in his bedroom, which inspired her to write a book called *Emotional Superpowers: Empower a Child, Heal the World*. This gives kids the tools to fully express their pain and facilitate their healing.

A favorite bedtime routine of Wes' was to hear a story read. His favorite book, *Danny and the Dinosaur*, was also my favorite as a child. But during the first few weeks of mourning, I felt I did not have the strength to read one single word to him. I just didn't have it in me.

One night as I was putting him to bed, I tried to comfort him. He had been crying. My efforts were useless, as he continued to cry and then began screaming. Then he asked me for a drink of water. After I got him one, he threw it and told me, "It's the wrong cup!" Each time he would ask for something else, I would try to help him, yet my efforts just infuriated him more. He told me that everything I was doing was wrong.

My poor little boy did not know how to express his sadness and could not understand why his world had been torn apart. *Why was Mommy crying so much? Where was Daddy?*

Finally, Wes turned to Rachelle and said to her, "I'm mad at you!" I pulled him into my body and replied, "Why are you mad? She isn't mad at you. Mommy isn't mad at you either. I love you." After a few moments of embracing him, he settled down.

I was able to read Wes' favorite dinosaur book to him as Rachelle encouraged me with every word. With a prayer in my heart, I cradled him in my arms until he fell fast asleep.

TWENTY-SIX

....

ATTENDING dōTERRA CONVENTION

I made the very difficult decision to attend the annual convention of dōTERRA, the essential oils company that I was working with just a few short weeks following Wade's passing. I had not intended to go. But Wade had been integral in getting me involved in this business, and I saw the convention as an opportunity to honor him and to show up for the people who had known him who were colleagues of ours. Years before, Wade had had a strong impression that we needed to really look seriously at this business. After meeting with the CEO, he told me, "This is the right company. I trust the owners. They are good people."

Making the hour-long drive to the convention center in downtown Salt Lake City through traffic, the constant flow of tears, and being alone was almost too much to bear. For many years, we had sat together at these conventions. I would now sit alone. Name tags would reserve our seats: "Wade and Laura Holbrook." Thousands of people were part of our marketing team. We were leaders. They knew us as a power couple. We had set company records together! The many years of mood swings and mental illness were not known among our business associates. Together we had built a very successful team working around the world.

How I dreaded people coming up to me and asking how I was doing just one month after his passing! I had a dear friend, Kalli, who was asked to be one of the keynote speakers in front of 30,000 people in the audience. She asked if she could share my story of the blessing that this business had been for my family during this difficult time and the kindnesses that had been shown us. We had meals brought to our doorstep that came from many leaders, and we received gift baskets from the company containing messages of hope. One such message was "Be Brave" written on a large wooden board. I placed this within eyeshot of my daily routine. I received uplifting and caring texts from one of the executives almost daily.

Because I had received the spiritual download not to let my suffering go to waste, I willingly agreed to let my friend share my story during her keynote. "If this can give just one person hope," I said, "I want you to describe it. I will trust, and I will do something so hard if it would inspire others to continue to take one step forward every moment of every day!" After granting permission, I decided to attend the convention.

As I made my way to my seat on arrival, I noticed that the name tags read, as I had guessed they would, "Wade and Laura Holbrook." There were clearly two seats reserved. By then, I was accustomed to crying. Surprisingly, however, I didn't burst into tears at that moment. It wasn't until my friend Lassen locked eyes with me and left her seat next to her husband to come to sit by me that I lost composure. She put her arm around me and held me.

There are people that listen to the gentle promptings of Spirit and will respond. I call them earthly angels. Lassen is one of them.

It was a bit surreal to listen to Kalli sharing my story from the stage. I felt a combination of gratitude, desperation, sadness, loneliness, and pain then and during the rest of that convention. Many loving friends freely gave of their love and prayers.

The drive home alone that night was accompanied by a flood of tears. Everything felt foreign. It was warm outside, and the smell of car exhaust fumes filled the air, which only added to the emptiness I was experiencing. It felt cleansing to me to cry loudly. I would feel a sob coming up and allow it to fully release.

Many years earlier, I had made a promise to my Father in heaven. At the time, we were struggling to pay our bills due to a failed business startup. I said: "Father in heaven, if you bless me again with abundance, I will always remember where it comes from. It all comes from thee."

After Wade's passing, many people asked me what I would do for money and if I needed help. A tremendous tender mercy from my Father in heaven was that I didn't need to be concerned about supporting my family. I had a residual income from something Wade, and I had built together. Heavenly Father was indeed preparing a way for my family starting years earlier.

TWENTY-SEVEN

....

WADE'S JOURNAL

Shortly after Wade's passing, I received his belongings, including a journal. This helped me to recognize that we are all children of our loving heavenly Father. Wade was, and is, as much loved as I am, and I was loved as much as him.

One of the things I learned while reading his journal was that Wade experienced a miracle during his darkest hours. In his words, written while in the psych hospital:

Blessings,

I felt I was going to die. The drugs in and out of my system were killing me. I was locked in a psych unit for the second time, and I did not sleep for several days because of the new meds. My lips were getting tingly, and I thought I might be getting [unintelligible]. I felt I was getting impaired. Everyone thought I was either being manipulative or seeking attention. That made things even worse. *Knowing I would be up all night, I prayed to God to save me.*

After several hours God showed me the sphere of darkness that exists within my heart. It was filled with selfishness and sin. I realized I need to uproot it from my heart but was shown that it would be hard for me to remove it.

I felt the weight of the hands of angels on my head as they blessed me. I could see them when I closed my eyes. They were all in white with gray hair. They looked like twins, and their faces were ageless. They could have been anywhere from twenty to forty in age; it was hard to tell. They said nothing but their hands comforted me through the night. God sustained me for a purpose I do not yet know.

I was shown that if I took my life, I would not find peace on the other side.

While reading this passage in Wade's journal, I received a download from the Spirit. The next life is a continuum from this life. Whatever addictions or appetites we have in this life will continue in the next. Who we become in this life—our character—is that which remains in us. Therefore, love God and your neighbor. It is imperative that we come to know the Savior now. He is ready with open arms!

I continued to receive downloads through the Spirit that Wade was not instantly "at peace" when he crossed over. His journey continued from where he was when he left us.

Many months before, he had started experiencing brain fog and fatigue. It seemed to be getting worse. I remember how he had to sit down multiple times at Brianna's wedding to Shay because of fatigue and dizziness. Doctors were not able to identify the physical issue. He had gone about every other week to the ER with strange symptoms. I do not know if the cause was withdrawal from pain pills or something else. Attention was on him continually. He exhibited addict-like behavior. At times, I felt his physical complaints were attempts to gain attention.

Wade was a paradox. On the one hand, he would offer to serve. On the other, he would retreat and exhibit selfish behaviors. I could not predict anything he did.

TWENTY-EIGHT

I COULD NOT SAVE HIM

I used to wonder what was going through Wade's mind when he was in the bathtub. At what point did he know that he had gone too far and wouldn't be rescued? Thoughts of his final moments would haunt me for quite some time. *I should have texted him that day when I had the feeling to do so. I should have told him that it would be OK, and he was loved.*

About two weeks after his passing, my therapist reassured me that it was not my fault. Before then, I felt burdened by unbearable guilt. She told me, "I would have stopped the session if I felt you were somehow abusing him, or that he was abusing you." With kindness and tears, she held me for several minutes as I shook and cried. "How can this be real?" I asked her. "We were just here with you. And now, here I am again. Alone with my therapist."

My therapist spent the next two hours with me as I sobbed and vented my emotions. She reminded me of what I chose my role to be as his wife—a savior of some sort. I couldn't fix him. I couldn't save him. "This is not your role anymore," she told me. "Take care of yourself. Take care of your children now."

The day was warm as I walked out of her office. I noticed the feeling of the sun on my face. The sun still rose and set each day. I got into my car and drove home. I did internalize that it wasn't my fault that day. She was there with me the last time I was with him. In my utter desperation, I had to trust her. I released my guilt that day.

TWENTY-NINE

....

WALKING AND STUDYING

It was midafternoon when I decided to go for a walk. My phone was charged, and my headphones attached. I queued up commentaries about people who'd had near-death experiences so I could find out what they saw. I'd become quite obsessed with studying the afterlife.

After Shay had passed, I read every book I could get my hands on regarding near-death experiences. As I read them, I shared many comforting truths with Wade. One idea I'd read is that when we pass our spirits are tangible. We can embrace. There are cities on the other side just as there are here on earth. Everyone is busily working on very important things on the other side! Another report said that special clothing is prepared for "newbies" who have just crossed over. And just as there is clothing, there are those assigned to make the

175

clothing! Everything testifies of a loving Father in heaven. All things—even inanimate objects—are alive and testify. Wood, stone, trees, animals are all created for us and to glorify our Father in heaven.

At the time, we had a set of stairs that went up from the kitchen. Our kitchen was very large as we had knocked out the wall that separated it from the dining area. Two rooms became one. This was my dream kitchen because it had ample room for family get-togethers. Wade's favorite place to sit was on the third step from the bottom because it was the central place where many conversations happened. I could remember him sitting on the stairs as if it was yesterday and telling me, "Laura, don't doubt that Shay lives on. I know that he does just as much as I know that I am sitting here now." It was so crazy to think that now Wade was gone! How much I wanted to know exactly what Wade was experiencing!

I am sure that my Father in heaven was tired of me asking for another sign! But I longed for reassurance. I continued to pray for answers and comfort.

My walk that day turned into a very long walk. I found respite from my emotional suffering with exercise. One of the ways that I coped with my grief was to feel my physical body. Feeling the heat, the hunger, and the thirst was a distraction from the pain. An escape. I often found myself wishing that I was an old woman so that I would be closer to entering the spirit world. It felt like an emotional cleanse to push my body. I called it *sweat therapy*. On many occasions, my sweat would be accompanied by tears.

Day by day, my lifestyle consisted of hours of prayer and pure grit. I felt as if I had to put on my armor and had my sword ready to battle the crushing emotional pain. I had made a choice not just to survive but to live fully. In the early workouts shortly after his passing, I felt the encouragement from the other side of the veil. At the gym, the flood of tears was difficult to hide, so I shared my story with a few people who became good friends of mine. They would encourage me to press on. One friend told me that when I walked into the gym, there was light all around me. I was surrounded both by friends on this side of the veil and the other side.

I continued to pray for physical, emotional, mental, and spiritual strength. It was granted. I rarely was sick. I had the strength of my mind. I felt the calmness that only the spirit can bring.

Great comfort was found through music as well. I love all kinds of music. However, I found the most comfort in my new favorite song, "I Know That My

Redeemer Lives," penned by the Reverend Samuel
Medley in 1775.[3]

1.

I know that my Redeemer lives.
What comfort this sweet sentence gives.
He lives, He lives who once was dead.
He lives, my ever-living Head.
He lives to bless me with His love.
He lives to plead for me above.
He lives my hungry soul to feed.
He lives to bless in time of need.

2.

He lives to grant me rich supply.
He lives to guide me with His eye.
He lives to comfort me when faint.
He lives to hear my soul's complaint.
He lives to silence all my fears.
He lives to wipe away my tears.
He lives to calm my troubled heart.
He lives ALL blessings to impart.

3.

He lives my kind, wise heavenly friend.
He lives and loves me to the end.

He lives and while He lives, I'll sing.
He lives my Prophet, Priest and King.
He lives and grants me daily breath.
He lives, and I shall conquer death.
He lives my mansion to prepare,
He lives to bring me safely there.

4.
He lives! All glory to his name!
He lives, my Savior, still the same.
Oh, sweet the joy this sentence gives:
"I know that my Redeemer lives!"
He lives! All glory to his name!
He lives, my Savior, still the same.
Oh, sweet the joy this sentence gives:
"I know that my Redeemer lives!"

THIRTY

....

CHOOSING THE HEADSTONE

Choosing the headstone for Wade's grave felt like climbing a steep mountain. For support, I phoned my dear friend Melissa and asked her to come with me. She said she would meet me and Brianna at the monument store.

Upon hearing of Wade's death, Melissa was guided spiritually to find and print a certain photograph. She did not remember seeing it before but was shown it in her mind. And she was told to write on it "Guardian Angels." I had many dark hours in the first week of bereavement. One of darkest also became one of the sweetest. I was touched when Melissa knocked on my bedroom door at midday just days after Wade's passing to lovingly hand me this photo. It was the photo of Wade helping Shay put on his tie just before marrying Brianna. She had found it on Wade's Facebook page.

I cherished that photo and kept it close to me, holding it as I walked around the house. Somehow it made both men feel closer to me in my time of mourning.

With Melissa's help, I would face this day with courage. I wasn't alone. I felt surrounded by angels.

Brianna rode with me. During the car ride, we discussed how this visit felt all too familiar given that we had just chosen a headstone for her husband a few months earlier. Shay was so young. He had loved Monster drinks, Xbox, and Cheetos. His headstone fit was a beautiful dark gray stone that had a slight sparkle, and the tribute suited him perfectly. I hoped we would be able to come up with a similarly perfect tribute for Wade. The monument store was fifteen miles from our home in which we lived with all of my children. Brianna had sold her home to move back in with me after Shay's death for emotional support. The drive was mixed with shock and stomachaches and the desire to put this moment behind me.

Wade's burial place was currently marked with a temporary stand with a small granite square plate indicating his name and his birth and death dates. This would soon be replaced with a customized headstone. What a strange business! There is such a sense of finality to the matter of laying a headstone over a burial ground. I started bargaining with God. *If we don't put a headstone down, then things could be taken back. I can still go back in time and change something.*

I knew these thoughts were not logical, but somehow, they entered my mind. *Can't I just go back in time? This didn't really happen. This wasn't what I chose or wanted.*

And then we were there, again. We had arrived. The grounds at the store were covered with examples of different types of headstones from which to choose. We took a quick look then headed inside.

There were large windows at the front of the store. It was a sunny day, and I was grateful for the sunshine that came through them.

Three unmatched metal chairs were set out in front of a large wooden desk. We took our seats, Melissa, Brianna, and I sat down and waited. My stomach was in knots.

"May I help you?" asked the older gentleman seated behind the desk. His face was familiar. Recognizing the same people from just a few months earlier was difficult. I was glad to remember that this man was kind.

"I need to choose a headstone for my husband," I replied. This was followed by a flood of tears.

On a single sheet of paper, the salesman drew out the basic shape of the monument. We had chosen a large, beautiful stone with a brown undertone. Then the words began to form. "Larry Wade Holbrook," it would read. Birthdate and death date. A color photo was chosen to be placed at the center top of the headstone. This picture was taken during the summer at a lively family reunion. Wade's smile was contagious. He beamed! He was wearing a red shirt, and his skin was a golden tan. He looked so happy and handsome! For an image, we decided on an etching of the Salt Lake Temple with tulips encasing the bottom. Everything had meaning.

A week earlier, my second eldest daughter, Caitlyn, had a special moment, which she relayed to me, "Mom, I was driving when I felt very strongly that I needed to go a different direction. I didn't know where I was driving or why and just ended up at a Christian bookstore. I walked in and saw this painting, and I was told to buy it for you." She had felt the presence of her dad directing her. The painting she bought was of the Salt Lake Temple with tulips. The colors were bright and vibrant. It was hung in our living room just days after his passing. It felt perfect that this image would be etched into his headstone.

....

THIRTY-ONE

THE FIRST YEAR AFTER LOSS

By the two-month mark, I was tired of crying, tired of being sad. I longed for the first year to be over. From grieving for Shay, I knew that the first year is full of constant reminders and heartache. With each new season, memories flood your mind of the times spent together. Now, as the summer ended, a new mourning process took place. It was as if a giant boulder came crashing down a steep mountain terrain and landed on our household. Whether you wanted it or not, it was coming, and it wasn't pretty. It was rough. It was painful.

I tried to distract myself by always keeping busy and moving. Scattered throughout was the cold realization of what had happened. Wade and Shay were gone. There was not a day that there was not someone crying in our home. It wasn't just about me. My children were impacted and mourning too. My heart ached when little Grace had a Daddy/daughter event at her school, and her dad was not there to go with her. And little Wes could not grasp the concept of death, so he kept asking when Daddy would come back.

When I would look into my children's innocent eyes and see resemblances of him, it slew me. My son has his dad's hands. He has his side profile.

And the painful reminders did not just occur day by day; they came hour by hour and minute by minute. I did my best to follow the advice I had given to Brianna shortly after Shay's passing. "Can you make it through the next minute? The next minute after that? Breathe deeply, take a drink of water, and eat that bite of food. Do not give care to tomorrow or next week," I told her. "You will be provided for next week. Every day will unfold, and you will be given what you need when you need it. You have the Creator of the entire universe on your side. He has you under His care."

Years before, when I was stressed about lack of money because of a failed startup business, Wade shared an inspiring song with me, "Consider the Lilies," whose lyrics were inspired by the following passage from the Bible (Matthew 6: 27–29):

Which of you by taking thought can add one cubit unto his stature?

And why take ye thought for raiment? Consider the lilies of the field, how they grow; they toil not, neither do they spin . . .

The song fast became one of my favorites, and it still is to this day. I love the message it conveys. Lilies don't worry about tomorrow. They just grow and know God will provide everything they need to reach their full potential: sun, earth, moisture, and more. It means: Don't worry about what tomorrow will bring, just trust God.

Because it reminded me so heavily of my life with Wade, I found it extremely difficult to listen to at first. However, I mustered enough courage and played it anyway and embraced the tears and the memories of our life together—even the painful ones. Listening to it, I was comforted. Despite his mental illness, he was giving me the message not to worry. Father in heaven always provides.

Blessed by this song, I was reminded that I knew my Savior personally. He walked with me.

THIRTY-TWO

....

AN EXCERPT FROM MY JOURNAL

God was patient with me during my journey of healing—as he is with us all. In my journal, I wrote:

It has been seven months ten days since his passing. I am walking through the valley of the shadow of death and sorrow because at times I find myself leaning on things I know will not being me lasting peace. I find myself seeking out distractions so that I do not have to fully feel the pain of the past year. I understand true grief, pain, and loss. The moments of "feeling" bring up emotions, and I sob uncontrollably.

Two days ago, I felt quite down as it was our twenty-third anniversary. I recalled the day that I knew our marriage was over. No amount of M&Ms was going to fill the painful void that I felt. I was thinking, I deserved this. How could I bear this burden? The weight of responsibility I felt in every area of my life was crushing. I once again faced a choice... light or darkness?

I chose to go for a run outside in the sunshine. The sun is so therapeutic. My favorite route passed the road where the cemetery is. Over and over, I found myself emotionally crumbling. My sunglasses fogged up, and I had to continually remove them to wipe the lenses so that I could see again. I listened to my favorite classic rock music. And I did my best to motivate myself, thinking, I got this. I can be strong. I will sweat out the pain. I looked up to the sky and pleaded for strength from God. Immediately I was given it and felt more energy. I am learning to appreciate these tender mercies. Much of the time, the weight of the loss is crushing. It awes me and takes my breath away when I understand the significance of the loss of Wade.

I wasn't sure if I should stop by the cemetery on this anniversary. As I approached the road, the pain was too great, so I kept running along my usual route. Another mile or so later, I felt the need to turn back. The sun was beginning to set. Golden hour. I found myself desperately running toward the cemetery. Cars passed me. Everyone is busy with their normal lives, I thought. They don't know why I am crying and running.

I began to pick up the pace, almost as if I would get to sit with Wade and have a conversation. Within minutes, I was there. I collapsed. I ran my fingers over the lettering that spelled his name. I gently rubbed the hard water stains from the photo of him on the headstone. He looked so handsome.

The grass in the cemetery was so green today. Pear trees in bloom lined the walkways. A beautiful hand statue depicting the Resurrection stands in the center. Majestic Utah mountains surround the grounds. I paid special attention to the sensation of the sun warming my face, my tears running down my cheeks, my heart racing from the run, the cool grass. And I found respite in the physical sensations. I didn't even mind the slight pain I felt from the foot I had broken just a week before Christmas because it was a slight distraction from the real and very raw pain of my loss. The pain of being alone. Alone in my thoughts. Alone in raising my six kids. Someone without a partner.

THIRTY-THREE

....

SUCH A BEAUTIFUL DATE

At Christmas that year, our first Christmas without Wade, I drew my sword energetically and began cutting myself free of the pain. With that sword, I carved a new path for myself and my kids. We would do things differently. We had to. My determination was a combination of pure grit and getting on my knees.

Christmas morning, which fell on a Sunday that year, we drove through the snow to our local IHOP for pancakes. In years past, Wade would make an egg breakfast while I made smoothies and pancakes for the kids. I would never have considered eating at a restaurant. But I was determined to find joy in the smallest things and do things differently, like eating out and making the meal fun.

Winter came and went. The buds on the trees were showing signs of new life. Grief hit hard in April. Grieving was not a pretty package wrapped in gift wrap, enabling me to go through each stage of grieving neatly and then on to the next phase. The process was messy, and many times, embarrassing. I often cycled back to denial or anger. At times I would feel weak. Other times, I felt I had the courage of a lion. Every day was different. I embraced the anger, the tears, the sadness, the joy. Faced with pain, I always had a choice.

In the spring, I started going out on dates with men. Partly this was for a distraction from the pain. But it was also to give myself hope that one day, I would have companionship and a true connection with another human being. I wanted to love and be loved. Wade and I had been on track for a divorce when he committed suicide. I had been lonely in my marriage for many years. Now I craved touch and genuine connection. I was tired of sleeping alone, attending social events and family events alone. While I wasn't technically "alone," considering that I was surrounded by kids and extended family, I felt lonely without a partner.

I recall visiting my parents one evening. As an avid genealogist, my mom preserves and displays many photos of deceased ancestors and current family photos.

Casually, I began thumbing through some of these. When I came across the birth announcement for Wes from three years earlier, a flood gate opened, and tears hit me with great force. It was a folding announcement that had ample room for multiple photos. I ran my fingers over each photo. There was Wade holding his infant son while I beamed at them, witnessing this miracle. My thoughts then went to my complete loneliness and despair.

Grief is like waves in an ocean. Over time, the waves become further apart, but when they hit, they could be as strong as on the day a loss happened. I ached for companionship. This was something I had always longed for—a together family. I wanted to be happy. I wanted a connection with my spouse!

Because of Wade's addictions, there was a disconnect between us much of the time. Our intimate life was spotty. For years I had blamed myself for this and thought it must have been me that was the problem, that perhaps I wasn't pretty or skinny enough. I was defective. And yet I remained. I had been stuck in the false belief that I needed to put my "eternal family" and commitment to marriage above all else, including listening to my own intuition!

While I was accustomed to sobbing loudly in the privacy of my car or closet, here, my feelings were exposed. My sweet mother asked me, "Laura, what do I do? Oh dear! I want to help, but I don't know what to do." She began to cry with me. She then called my brother, and within ten minutes, he was with me. Along with my dad, he offered to administer a blessing to me.

I do recall that blessing and the peace I felt afterward, as it helped me to embrace that flood of emotions that was my path to healing. I welcomed the quiet comfort that came from being blessed, which allowed my tears to dry up. The warmth of pure JOY came over my body.

In the blessing from God that came through my brother, I was promised that I would not be alone very much longer and that the Lord was preparing someone for me.

While I certainly looked forward to the day of joining my life with the man who was being prepared for me, I was also keenly aware that this man would not "complete" me. I knew that I was enough and that my savior, Jesus Christ, was the individual that completed me. He was always there and would never leave me!

We are intended to have companionship. We are not created to be alone! We are created to experience joy in life!

Three months from that day, I would meet Matt for our first date. God indeed knew what he was doing when some other guys I thought I would really like were kept from me. Before I met Matt, my experiences of dating could be compared to mixing oil and water. It just didn't make sense!

During this time of dating, my sister Amanda became my "Lucy," like in the Peanuts comic strip, I confided in her and shared stories of going out with different guys. She was baffled that these connections didn't pan out. Then one day, a strong feeling came over her, and she abruptly exclaimed, "Heavenly Father is preparing someone for you, so you should not worry about the other nonsense."

Everyone has her own path. I knew in my heart that it was not my path to be single very long. God knew exactly what I needed and gave it to me when I needed it. Over and over, I was reminded to surrender control and trust my journey.

Being resistant at first, I finally decided to create an online dating profile after my sister told me she had a feeling that I needed to! Matt and I matched up. I liked that he messaged me right away, saying, "Let's meet." At that moment, we were having a large family gathering at my sister's home. Excitedly, I showed my mom his picture. She immediately asked, "How tall is he?" "Six foot four," I replied. We both thought he was very handsome!

I found myself a few days later sitting across from Matt at a breakfast bar. We'd agreed to meet in a public place for an hour on a Saturday morning. He had accidentally slept in, and when I called his cell to ask if he was still coming, I actually woke him up. Without hesitation, he threw on the closest shirt he could find, a pair of jeans, his brown cowboy boots, and raced to the location. He apologized to me profusely, exclaiming that he never sleeps in. I had read all the dating books I could get my hands on during the previous months. I decided to go against all the advice I had read that being late was a bad sign. I wanted to meet him even though he was late.

As we sat across from each other, enjoying our açai bowls, I felt peace and had a sense of comfort that felt like "home." The moment I met Matt was the moment that my appetite returned. My heart continued to heal. Since Shay passed away over a year earlier, I'd not had much desire for food. After a few moments, Matt held my chair, and lovingly slid it closer to his. Then we engaged in a very real conversation. He was so easy to talk to! I felt so comfortable. It is hard to put into words exactly, but with him, I was enough. There were no guessing games. Everything just flowed. He looked into my eyes in those first few moments and said, "You are flawless." I will always cherish that moment.

We shared life stories. I told him about my marriage to Wade. I shared with him who I was. I shared my pain and sorrows. Much to my surprise, I finished my entire meal, and it was delicious! We had spent just under an hour together when he gently gave me a kiss goodbye. He stepped back into his large white pickup truck and said that he would call to see me again.

THIRTY-FOUR

....

BLESSINGS FULFILLED

With Matt, everything flowed naturally. It felt easy! My eyes were wide open this time. I was no longer living in "the should" or with a checklist. I wanted real. I wanted honesty—even if it meant learning of imperfections. On our second date, he shared with me his pain about past relationships and how he questioned everything. He told me how he'd followed what he thought was the right path, only in the end feeling hurt and alone. He exited his marriage of eleven years.

Two years had passed since that time. He felt disillusioned with the dating world and had resolved that there must not be a person out there with whom he would completely connect.

I was intrigued by him. I thoroughly "stalked" him on social media, finding out who his friends were, what he posted, and most importantly, who he was. I shared every little detail about Matt leading up to this point with my sister Amanda. She kept telling me, "I have a good feeling about him, Laura."

Added to my prayers was that of wanting to find a man who would not only be good for me but also for my children, as they no longer had a father anymore. It would take a special and patient man to help to heal their hearts and together with me, pick up the pieces from the devastation that Wade had wrought.

I made a list of characteristics that I desired in a mate and posted it on my mirror. Intelligent, a keen sense of humor, out-of-the-box thinker, entrepreneur, adventurous, tall with large hands (I have a thing for hands), has had children of his own (because he would understand the love a parent has for his/her child), and the exact age range of thirty-seven to forty-six.

It was spring 2017 when I drove to Matt's home for the first time, all the while praying that if this man was for me, I would feel it. I wanted to receive clear confirmation! I knew that I found him very handsome, but that wasn't enough for me. I wanted it all. I wanted in a man what was on my mirror—every detail! He needed to be kind, hardworking, and self-less, among many other qualities. I wouldn't settle for any less.

While I wasn't naïve, in my heart I was certain that I could have it all. I had already received an answer directly from heaven that someone was being prepared for me! I had faith. There is no better way to describe that feeling—other than as *faith.*

I could feel, without a doubt, that Wade was working on my happiness from the other side and wanted me not to be alone much longer. Many downloads came to me. It was as if Wade were continually communicating with my spirit. Thoughts would come to me at the most random times that were so clear!

I would not be alone. Aloneness was not my path. Even so, well-meaning people would give me unsolicited advice about my marital status. Some would say, "You need to be single for two years before you can marry again," or "You couldn't possibly be ready for a relationship this soon." I also heard, "Don't focus on yourself at all, put everything into the kids." They didn't get it. My entire life was my kids. I had shelved and ignored myself for years while my intuition was screaming at me to hold better boundaries. How could these people understand me if they had not walked in my shoes?

What I have learned is that my path is not any other's path. His is not mine. My Father in heaven knows my heart and my deepest desires, and he guides me. I finally had learned to listen to my voice. I was done with doing things to please other people. Even if it meant dating six months after Wade's passing to lift my spirits, I would take the criticism and secret disapproval! My past road was one of a lonely marriage. I was sick of being alone! At the time of my husband's death, we had lived apart for five months. And yet, even when he had been living at home, there had been loneliness. There was a disconnect. And that was no way for me to continue living anymore.

I have the gift of hearing the spirit! The moment I get on my knees, I have the attention of an angelic being on assignment for the Father. My guardian angel speaks to me. As I prayed for the right man for my family, I trusted that God would provide him.

As I pulled into the neighborhood where Matt lived, feelings of excitement and intrigue entered my heart. I found his home, parked my car in his short, steep driveway, and walked up the sidewalk to knock on a large wooden front door.

He had just returned from a short trip to California where he and his daughters had stayed at a beach house. He surfed while they gathered shells and splashed in the ocean. Matt adores his girls and is a doting father!

We had only met a few weeks earlier. Each time he had sent me a text or a photo of himself with the girls playing at the beach, my heart jumped! I couldn't wait for him to return!

On his last day surfing, his leash broke and the board got away from him. He frantically swam to retrieve it from the rushing waves. Unfortunately, in so doing, he threw his back out. He downplayed the injury, but later I learned that throughout the twelve-hour drive home, he had been in excruciating pain.

Before I left for his home, I gathered several essential oils to bring that I knew would help him heal. Upon arriving at his front door and knocking, he called me on my cell and said just to walk in as he could not move from his bed. He was laid out flat.

I entered his beautiful home. In the entryway hung a large photo of the Salt Lake Temple. A sturdy wooden chair was offset by a very thick, tall, floor-to-ceiling mirror. The rug in the entry was lush, yet simple. He clearly liked quality and comfort. His home was well kept.

I made my way up the carpeted staircase and entered his room where I found him lying flat on his back as he'd described. Our eyes met. A flood of feelings came over me in that very moment. I knew that he was my man. We joke about it now because he wasn't able to get ready for me to come over. His hair was disheveled, and he wore a tee-shirt and pajama pants. I smiled at him and walked closer to his bedside. Enthusiastically I then presented him with the oils and informed him that I would be applying them to his injured back.

He willingly obliged my ministrations. We spent the afternoon laughing, sharing, and getting to know each together. It was a turning point for us. I had received the answer to my prayers. The rest is history, as they say.

Every step felt easy and natural, something I had never experienced before. I met his best friends from childhood and got to know his family well during a trip to Montana on which my kids and I stayed with his entire family at their cabin on the lake. Our kids quickly became best friends.

Deciding to marry was the next natural and logical step.

I didn't care how we would marry. I didn't give a hoot about coordinating colors, flowers, clothes, or anything else temporal for that matter! I knew I just wanted to be with him! His touch brought me a feeling of such peace and comfort. I felt safe. I trusted him. I adored this man!

I knew he was sent from God, and my eyes were wide open.

My heart was healing.

Wearing blue jeans, we eloped in our small town with a simple ceremony. It was a beautiful moment! My friend Steve married us standing on the freshly cut lawn outside a local church. The ceremony was beyond simple. It was just us, him and two witnesses—Steve's wife and Matt's friend Andreas. We kept it a secret from everyone, including our kids, that we had married for the following four weeks.

At the time of this writing, it has been two years since we married. Every time Matt holds my hand, I feel comfort. My heart is whole. I know what it feels like to be loved by a man I trust completely. His hands are strong, capable, and larger than mine! He is humble, kind, gentle, and yet strong and fierce, like a lion. He has care and concern for each of my children that is the concern of a father. And he sees things—spiritually. Matt will get feelings out of nowhere. These will at times wake him up during the night. "This child needs this . . . or that . . ." he'll tell me. I know that he is guided, just as a father would be in raising his own biological children.

It is said that no one is "perfect." I do believe, however, that two people can be perfect for each other. We understand each other. He even longs to know who Wade was. A big part of my healing came from being able to mourn with my husband, Matt.

Matt will ask me about Wade. I have shared so much about Wade that Matt feels like he knows him. I tell him that they would have been friends in this life. In my heart, I do believe that they made agreements with each other before coming to earth.

THIRTY-FIVE

....

JOURNEY TO PERU

Matt's childhood friend Jimmy is an adventurous traveler. He told Matt that out of the top one hundred experiences in his life, ninety-five occurred in Peru and, more specifically, in the Amazon jungle. Out of curiosity, I asked him to share details.

Jimmy told us of the personal growth he had experienced by visiting with shamans in the jungle who work with plant medicine. Feeling guided to learn more, I conducted some research online and discovered that many people who do traditional ceremonies with indigenous shamans living in these remote natural areas report incredible deep healing from trauma and addiction.

Through my studies, I learned about the plant medicine Ayahuasca that is made from an Amazonian vine. When consumed, people go into a trance state and have healing visions. Scientifically, people suffering from severe depression have shown measurable improvements in their brain scans after having an experience with Ayahuasca. The locals call it Mother Ayahuasca because it is believed to be a feminine spirit. I read many first-person testimonials, and as I continued to learn the plant's healing properties, I was fascinated!

There are many misconceptions about plant medicine. Let's set the record straight. First and foremost, it is *not* for those that want to get "high" or abuse a substance. I myself have never smoked anything in my life, nor have I ever had the desire to alter my state for the purpose of an escape from my life or to get high. I don't consume alcohol or even coffee, which is a stimulant. I have never liked the feeling that pain pills give me, even if I am in pain, like after having surgery, and have been prescribed them! I do not take them.

What fascinated me about Ayahuasca were its healing properties, especially in regard to anxiety, grief, and PTSD. I can certainly attest to this fact in hindsight, as I do feel differently than I did prior to my trip Peru. In brief, after studying its effects, I resolved to go to the jungle and take Ayahuasca. I felt guided to go, although it would mean that I would be away from my little ones for nearly two weeks. The older kids could handle my absence fine, but the littlest kids would likely struggle with missing me when I was away. Even so, it felt like an opportunity for deep transformation. I longed for further healing and hoped for a bit more closure. Matt said he would accompany me. Bottom line, both Matt and I knew we needed to go.

There are preparations that must be done prior to consuming Ayahuasca, including adhering to a special diet for several weeks beforehand. The process requires letting go of physical appetites, much like fasting does.

Flight arrangements were made. We would drive to Las Vegas and then take a flight to Lima, Peru, and make a small connecting flight to Iquitos. The flight from Vegas left around 3 AM. This would mean we would need to leave home no later than 8 PM.

On a plain sheet of paper, I wrote down the numbers of days we would be gone. I stuck it to the fridge in the kitchen and told my little kids that each day they should cross off a number. Then, when all the numbers were crossed off, I would be home. I found myself continually reassuring my young kids and most especially my little boy. I took matching stickers from his car book and touched them together, telling him they had hugged and kissed and would be back to see each other. I then stuck one sticker on his shirt and one on mine. I trusted that these small concrete things would give him the confidence that he would see me soon when words weren't enough.

With bags packed, we hugged our kids goodbye and left. We had been driving for about two hours when a terrible snowstorm hit us. Visibility was so limited to about twelve inches in front of the Jeep we were driving in. The snow fell in large flakes propelled by huge gusts of wind. Temperatures dropped quickly, and the road surface rapidly became like a sheet of ice. We saw a few random cars pulling off to the side of the road and just stopping. As the road surface changed to a slight downward tilt, we began to feel the Jeep picking up speed. To avoid sliding out of control, Matt resisted applying the brakes and instead attempted to change to a lower gear. This shifting was not successful as hoped.

We began to slide sideways, crossing to the other side of the road and back again. It felt almost like slow motion. It was a miracle that there was no oncoming traffic! As we slid toward the guard rail, I closed my eyes tightly and braced for impact. To both of our astonishment, we didn't hit anything but slid back and forth, narrowly missing the guard rails on both sides of the road!

We slowly made our way through the storm until we reached to McCarran International Airport. Upon inspection of the jeep, we discovered that there was not even a scratch on it. Our prayers were answered. We were on our way.

THIRTY-SIX

....

ARRIVAL IN PERU

att's friend Jimmy greeted us warmly at Jorge Chavez International Airport in Lima. He had a wide, contagious smile. His dark hair was tussled and held back from his face with a hat that read: "Mind Astronaut." With such a guide, our trip would surely be an adventure! Draped over his shoulders was a large white scarf that I had guessed he'd bought on his previous trips to Peru. He was so enthusiastic about us coming with him! I was so touched when he offered his emergency seat row to us to give us ample legroom on the flight to Iquitos. Matt and I are both tall, so it was wonderful to have more legroom in the small plane! Feeling excited and a bit nervous, the flight took off.

The air was heavy with humidity. The sound of the "taxis" in Peru hummed through the streets. The taxis looked like large motorized tricycles. The driver sits in the single front seat and holds onto handlebars. The back seat for passengers consists of two tires and a very small wooden bench. There are no seat belts. You just hang on! The top is covered, resembling an old-fashioned buggy.

It didn't seem that there were rules in the streets. Lights would go from red to green, and then vehicles would rush to get through the intersection. Matt pointed out to me that the rickshaw running next to ours, which carried a mother with a very young baby had a flat tire. In fluent Spanish, he enthusiastically let the driver know. The driver acknowledged this and kept right on driving! The mother held her baby tightly, and the baby just jumped along with all the bumps unfazed.

I couldn't help but wear a huge smile on my face as this was a new adventure. With my blond hair blowing every which way and this huge grin, I looked exactly like the tourist I was. It was a different world.

A very healthy lunch was shared with our new friends. We would be with these individuals for the following ten days. There were ten of us, both couples and single women and men. Most in the group were American, but one couple was from Canada. Although from different walks of life, all of us were seeking similar healing: We were looking for peace from trauma, loss, and even abuse.

After leaving Iquitos, we traveled by van for two hours. The windows were down, hair was blowing wildly, and lots of laughter was erupting as we got to know each other better. At last, we reached the Amazon River. Approaching the river's edge, we got out of the van and stepped onto a longboat with a canopy top. The boat looked much like a canoe—but larger. The journey to our final destination continued. We could hear the hum of boats motoring along the Amazon on either side of us. The ride lasted about an hour.

The boat docked. From the shore, we looked upward to the lodge where we would be staying. There were very large wooden stairs that we would need to climb, with landings that led to the next set of stairs. The color of the steps was a brilliant red. This offset the very lush green leaves of the jungle. Leaves larger than an average man's torso hung on the trees and overhung the path leading to the main cabin where we would congregate as a group. The scene was utterly picturesque! I began taking photos. I even snapped a photo of Matt walking the ascending path, carrying our luggage.

Getting settled into our room, we saw that there was limited electricity (only from four in the afternoon to

six) or fans. Evens so, our accommodations were spectacular. Our bed was made of wood from the jungle, and white fabric netting to protect us from mosquitos was draped over the bedposts. It looked luxurious. To be in the middle of the jungle with a view that would be etched into my mind forever was a remarkable treat after a painful couple of years. Looking out the window, I again observed that the leaves of the plants were huge. They waved at me in the wind. It was a beautiful scene.

I realized very quickly that I was spoiled because I was accustomed to the modern conveniences of our western culture. Quite spoiled! The temperature of the air was very hot, and the humidity was oppressive. I would have killed for an air conditioner. There was no escape from the heat or humidity. Daily it rained buckets.

And the mosquitos loved me. At one point, I counted over forty bites from knee to ankle on one leg.

I have heard it said that the way to overcome fears of spiders and large bugs is to have exposure to them over and over. It's true. We had lots of little visitors in our room: bats, spiders, frogs, and thousands of mosquitos. The beautiful fabric that draped over the bed frame to completely encase the sleeping area was not just for looks; it was necessary. The buzzing sounds of hungry mosquitos could be heard all night long through the sheer fabric. By the end of the trip, I was much less freaked out by them than at the beginning. I inured myself to them.

The first night, we went by boat as a group to a village where we ate and drank authentic food, watched a dance, and then also participated in the dance with the local Peruvians. It was a lively evening! Sweat dripped from our pores as we danced, jumped, and twirled with the natives, laughing and feeling a release of tension. They eagerly offered us their homemade goods for sale—intricately woven pieces of artwork ranging from bracelets and necklaces to beautiful fans made of leaves. There were also very large insects that were preserved in glass bottles. As we chose each piece to purchase, we thought of our kids. These objects would surely be treasured for many years to come!

Leaving the small village required riding in very small, buggy-like taxi. We then rode a small boat back across the river that took quite some time to arrive at the lodge.

Preparing for the first ceremony meant that we could not consume any food past 2 PM that day. The ceremony would take place at night, and we needed empty stomachs. Let it suffice to say that the first ceremony we undertook could be compared to doing one hundred intensive therapy sessions all at once. By the end, I was exhausted. And I was changed.

Walking through the jungle in the middle of the night going to and from the main hall was never dull, to say the least! At one point, within two feet of our next step, sat one of the deadliest snakes in the jungle, a coral snake. Quickly we made our way around it with ample space. I was grateful for the sturdy boots I wore. I had only watched nature shows about the creatures we saw. I'd never seen one. We also witnessed a frog sparkling a bright purple color in the moonlight. With my headlamp secure, tall rain boots rising past my knees and wearing ample bug repellant, I would make my way through the darkness of the jungle with the group to the structure that was shaped much like an octagon.

With a thatched roof and up on stilts, this space was unique. Crude bathrooms were in a separate, much smaller area off of the main structure.

Two steps led up to the one door, which creaked when opened. It was lightweight and swung closed easily. Within the room were yoga mats laid out to match the shape of the room—all in a circle. By the looks of the room, it had been occupied many times before.

The Peruvians were kind and eager to help each of us feel comfortable. They were smaller in stature than us and yet their smiles—and their kindness—were larger than life.

For many in our group, this would be our first Aya journey. People from all walks of life—professionals, teachers, mothers and fathers, healers—we all came together for the purpose of healing, although each person's intention was very different from the rest. Some wanted closure from loss, and others wanted to understand who they were and their individual life purposes. One was there for help with physical ailments. One by one, we took turns sharing our intention for the first ceremony.

The amount of plant medicine I consumed was small, maybe a quarter cup. It tasted much like a mix of dirt and dark molasses and was very bitter. After everyone had their turn, we returned to our individual mats and waited quietly. I took this opportunity to meditate and pray intently to my Father in heaven, asking Him to please guide and help me. I was nervous and had no idea that my experience would be as intensely difficult as it would be.

The plant medicine began to work in my body after I'd been meditating for roughly twenty minutes. At that moment, our shaman began to sing a special improvised song, an *icaro*, which was the most beautiful, emotionally healing music. It was as if she was singing directly to me. The icaros, or sacred healing songs, work directly with the plant medicine, which is receptive to your specific healing needs.

The jungle was a hospital for healing the soul.

THIRTY-SEVEN

....

THE FIRST CEREMONY

The veil became very thin when the shaman sang her icaro. It became very real to me that I was a spiritual being having a human experience. I saw that I had existed long before my time on earth. I knew who I was.

I saw myself as a large bird, an angel-bird, strong, and majestic. Some might say that this bird is my spirit animal. Personally, I interpret the vision as a symbol of my character and the situation in which I found myself. I saw myself looking down over a great valley from a height. I was shown that even though I was rising above the world, I had a broken wing. Most importantly, I grasped that if I had complete faith and trust when I spread my wings, it would be then—in that very moment—that I would heal.

I could feel who I was before I came to earth to dwell in my physical body. My soul had a spiritual strength that I immediately recognized. The spirit was familiar. And there were no insecurities that I am not enough or any otherworldly concerns.

The voice that guided me was that of a female. Some call her Mother Earth. I understood she was kind and gentle and yet obeyed the laws of the great universe. My spirit knew that she was a servant of my heavenly Father. I was shown that some people get this wrong and that Mother Earth isn't pleased that the glory mistakenly goes to her and not to her creator. She would not exist if not for God.

In a massive spiritual "download," I was shown a series of truths: All things work in synchronicity according to the will of the father. All plants and animals and living things exist because of Him, and all things sing glory and praise to Him continually. There is so much we cannot see! There are worlds without number! The worlds are vast and cannot be described with earthly words! Our creator is love. None of us is ever alone. Whenever we ask, the servants of our Father in heaven on the other side of the veil are always ready to help us. But *we must ask* if they are to do so.

I was learning the true nature of God through the refiner's fire. He deeply loved me. He was keenly aware of my broken heart, yet He was refining me.

The intention I had set for the first ceremony was to experience healing from the passing of both Shay and Wade. Intense healing would follow. But I was told that it was not my place to ask for healing from my son-in-law's passing because we did not share "cords."

However, I could ask for healing from the pain that Wade caused me because *we* share cords. I was shown that Shay was fine and still involved with Brianna's life. Healing from Shay's death would be my daughter's journey.

I had never heard this term, *cords,* before. Upon researching it later, on the internet, I would learn that it is a reference to metaphysical energy that can connect two people's spiritual bodies. Sort of like an umbilical cord connects a mother to her unborn baby—but in a noncorporeal plane of existence.

By being shown these things I was then prepared for what was to come. I found myself standing in front of Wade. I am not sure exactly how much time passed as we communicated. I find it very difficult to put words that we use on earth to what transpired. The conversation was entirely telepathic, done from spirit to spirit.

My spirit began the exchange by expressing to him how badly he hurt me. I showed him different situations over the years, starting at the beginning of our marriage. I continued to show him the deep pain he caused me, expressing my sorrow, and it was excruciating. I cannot recall an occasion in my life when I have ever cried so many tears. This went on for about an hour, after which I paused and took a deep breath. I was exhausted.

I still find it very difficult to put into words what happened next, but I will do my best. Wade brought me to the moment when he made the decision to leave this earth. I was filled with such anger and disgust. Without words, I began to scream at him. "How could you do this to me?! And to our children?!" I asked, among other things. I was allowed to fully express everything I needed to say. Wade just listened. This phase of the journey seemed to last about twenty minutes, after which I began to settle down.

Wade's hand was outstretched toward mine. I reached for it. Now, after what seemed like a very long pause, he began to communicate with me. "Please let me go," his spirit said. "It's time. Cling to Matt. Matt was chosen for you. He will take care of you." I was shown that Matt and Wade knew each other in their pre-earth lives.

My heart ached. I replied, "I don't want to let go! I can't let go." He begged me. "But I love you still," I said.

The tears flowed like retained waters being released after a dam has broken. I saw Wade's face and his outstretched hand. I gathered all my inner strength, ready to forgive him. Suddenly, nausea was in full swing. The waves of this nausea were very strong. I begged Mother Earth to stop them, saying, "I don't want to throw up. I don't like to do that! I am out of control when I do that! It is gross! I'm afraid to let go!"

Mother Earth lovingly encouraged me to let go of the pain I felt attached to Wade, to purge it. I was shown that purging is a symbolic action, a sacrifice of sorts.

Finally, I was ready to let it all go, and I purged again. Then I felt even more exhausted.

It was the most emotionally cleansing experience I've ever had.

I have done many sessions of therapy related to my trauma over Wade and our unhappy marriage, and none compares to what transpired in the following moments. It was an intense experience. The best way I can describe it is that when I surrendered and purged the plant medicine (Ayahuasca) worked through my body to heal my spirit in every way. It was like doing a hundred sessions of therapy at one sitting.

My heart began to change. I shifted away from anger and pain. As the purging ended, I looked up and saw Wade, and I began to experience a perfect feeling of pure love and gratitude.

With hands still reaching toward each other's, I thanked him for everything, even for the pain he caused. I fully recognized that without the pain, I would not have grown. I would not be who I became if not for the pain. This was MY path, my life journey.

I am quite sure that my body was physiologically altered in that moment of forgiveness and gratitude. Over the years and in many of the therapy sessions I did for trauma recovery, from time to time I would say, "Everything happens for a reason" or "Pain helps me grow," but never did I feel the meaning of these words down to my very core. The experience transformed me at a deep spiritual level. Since then, I have not given so much as a thought to the idea that I am a "victim" of this type of trauma.

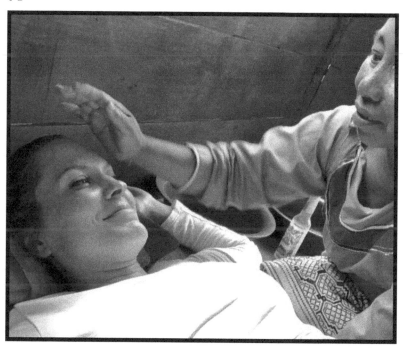

Toward the end of the ceremony, a very loving woman who was assisting the shaman began to work on the energy fields of my body, using reiki. This form of energy work was new to me and very soothing. Her hands remained inches from my stomach the entire time, and without touching my skin, I could feel her drawing out my emotional pain. There was a physical sensation as she did this and yet she didn't touch me!

The woman whispered to me that I was carrying a lot of pain and fear, and she swirled her hands in a pattern that literally made me feel more and more nauseous. Finally, I was ready to let it all go, and I purged again. Then I felt even more exhausted.

It was the most emotionally cleansing experience I've ever had.

THIRTY-EIGHT

···

THE SECOND CEREMONY

Because the first ceremony was thoroughly exhausting, I didn't think I could possibly do another. *I got what I came for,* I thought. It was as if I had just given birth, and the next day was being asked to do it again. I couldn't bear the thought of it. It was extremely draining!

I understood that this place in the jungle was a hospital for healing the spirit. That cleansing my spirit at this level was work. That taking Ayahuasca was not a recreational activity. However, I began making preparations to head back home. Among other things, I missed my "babies."

Then I learned that every ceremony is based on your intention and that no two ceremonies are alike. It took all the courage I had, but I opted in for another ceremony. I needed to face my issues head-on and be brave!

This time I asked for something much gentler. My intention was set. I would ask, "What is my mission in this life? What is my purpose?"

As soon as the plant medicine entered my body and took effect, I was told without hesitation, "Your mission is to show your children joy."

My spiritual download this time was intensely peaceful. With complete realization, I understood that showing my children joy was to live fully. I needed to press forward with faith despite feeling fear. Joy was on the other side of fear!

During the second ceremony, I felt heavenly light shining down upon me. I understood the sacredness of plant medicine. And that all living things, including the plants, sing glory and praise to the loving Creator. Plants are alive and sing glory to God. Our spirits are connected to theirs.

I was shown a brief glimpse of the afterlife. In this vision, I was standing in front of my older daughters. I held each one, cradled their beautiful faces in my hands, and kissed them. They looked roughly the same age as they currently were. Our spirits communicated perfectly—once again, telepathically. As usual, it is difficult to put into words, but if it would be something like, "We did it!" In this vision, I was their spirit sister. We had a connection that was eternal.

To them, I said, "I was chosen to be your mother on earth. I love you perfectly. We knew each other before we came to earth. We made agreements. Through pain, we grew in love. We did it!" We were finally on the other side—the place where we came from, home.

I saw their divinity. Their beauty was not of this world. I saw their strength. I saw their pain. I knew what it was in an instant. It was so deep that it literally took my breath away and brought tears to my eyes. I also was shown how their pain and suffering had a purpose.

My thoughts went to each of my kids in turn. I felt guilty for staying as long in my marriage as I did. I knew in an instant, that individually we could choose joy. It wouldn't come from accumulating things, status, or outer physical beauty. All was stripped from me. I could feel the heaviness of my body. My body was simple, a vessel for my spirit.

During the journey, I understood that I was being shown that the covenants I made with my Father in heaven were real. Being raised in a religiously conservative home, I have always believed in God. But I also subscribed to the belief that I had to "earn my way," and I never quite felt worthy enough! I didn't KNOW my creator. Throughout most of my married life, I went through the motions of doing what I thought was right because I believed that I would not be "enough" otherwise. Even though I wasn't outwardly sinning, I lived anxiously in the "shoulds."

Now, I understood perfectly that I was enough and that the purpose of life is growth. The variety of people we meet is meant to teach us about love.

I was learning the true nature of God as I was going through the refiner's fire. He deeply loved me. He was keenly aware of my broken heart and was refining me further.

In Revelation 3:18, it reads:

I counsel thee to buy of me gold tried in the fire, that thou mayest be rich . . .

In Zacharia 13:8–9, it reads:

And it shall come to pass, that in all the land, saith the Lord, two parts therein shall be cut off and die; but the third shall be left therein.

And I will bring the third part through the fire, and will refine them as silver is refined, and will try them as gold is tried: they shall call on my name, and I will hear them: I will say, It is my people: and they shall say, The Lord is my God.

In Job 23:10, it reads:

But he knoweth the way that I take: when he hath tried me, I shall come forth as gold.

THIRTY-NINE

....

THE FINAL CEREMONY

We are all worthy of God's love. At any moment, if we ask, God will be there for us. We are never alone.

During the last ceremony, I was shown a brief glimpse into the spirit world. The skies of this realm were a crystalline blue, and the mountain ranges were vibrant green and lush. I was shown, "Heaven is here," and that only my physical eyes prevent me from seeing it. However, If I practice opening my spiritual eyes, I will be able to see unparalleled beauty while alive on earth.

I will always remember the lessons I learned in the Amazon jungle, especially this one: As a human race, we are connected. We have more in common with one another than we do differences.

My body wasn't accustomed to the intense and humid heat, and I began to get a blister-like rash on the palms of my hands. I couldn't sleep at night because they itched something terrible! I feared that I had been bitten by something in the jungle. Because of urgency, I felt to get back home to a doctor, Matt and I left two days early. I sent pictures home by email of these strange blistery bumps to my family back home in Utah. My sister Heather shared that she had seen this with her missionary companions. When she served in Brazil on a church mission, many of her companions had to be sent home because their bodies could not tolerate the heat. I felt some relief, and it calmed my thinking to hear this fierce blistering might just be related to heat. This diagnosis was confirmed as we arrived at the airport in Iquitos, Peru. Inside a building with the air conditioning running, the blisters began to get smaller immediately. A day and a half later, we were home, and they were already nearly gone.

Arriving home to my babies was joyous! I held each of them tightly, cradled their faces, and kissed them— just as I had during the second Ayahuasca journey. I could see their essence. They are the beautiful children of our loving Father in heaven!

....

FORTY

JOY IS ON THE
OTHER SIDE OF FEAR

One of my greatest fears has been of the ocean. What I could not see beneath the surface of the water paralyzed me to the point that I would not enter so much as a lake unless it was crystal clear. The unknown in anything petrified me!

Then I married a surfer, a man who grew up, quite literally, in the ocean.

Surfing was Matt's love, his way to unwind, and he wanted to teach me to surf. I had a decision to make so I could enjoy this passion with him.

Just like facing the prospect of public speaking years ago and doing it despite my fear, I would face the ocean with the same determination. Having been raised in landlocked Utah most of my life, I had was always lived far from the coastline. I could count the times I had visited a beach on one hand.

While in California for a visit, we planned some time to surf. My daughter Caitlyn wanted to learn too. With a mutual friend teaching her and Matt teaching me, we entered the ocean. He was by my side, and with complete trust, I began following his instruction. I was determined to show my kids joy. I knew I must face my fears head-on as joy is always on the other side of fear!

I borrowed a wet suit, which was a bit too large, and learned the art of carrying the surfboard through the tiny waves near the shoreline. "Never turn your back to the ocean," Matt told me. As the water got deeper, I jumped onto the board. Lying on my stomach, I followed Matt's lead as he paddled his own board next to mine. As the waves began approaching, he showed me how to do what looked like a pushup on the board to allow the wave to pass under me. I had watched Matt "*duck dive*" previously. Duck diving is when you hold the front of the board and retain your breath and go under an approaching wave, allowing the water to rush over you. I imagined I would have swallowed a lot of the salty ocean attempting that.

I alternatively paddled my arms, right-left, right-left, making my way further out. I became so intensely focused on the technique he was teaching me that I nearly forgot about the unknown fish swimming below me! I was taken aback by the sunlight, offering me a perfect, sparkling reflection from every creature's movement in the vast ocean water. In one powerful wave, I spotted a school of small fish moving next to me!

Just as the waves became large enough to ride back to shore, Matt began instructing me on what to do. Go from lying on my tummy to sitting up quickly, then, while watching the ocean, begin turning my feet in the motion of an eggbeater. This motion would turn my board to face the shore. From there, I would return to my tummy and begin paddling as quickly as I could. I did this and got into position.

Matt then began very excitedly, telling me when to stand up. I managed to get up to my knees and balance for a few seconds, and then it felt like the ocean would swallow me up and spit me back out. On each attempt, I would emerge very tussled with the taste of salty water permeating my nose and throat. But I would laugh and felt the determination to do it again! This continued over and over.

Matt continued to teach me and encourage me. The wet suit kept me somewhat warm—except my hands and feet, which had begun to succumb to the freezing water.

I recall turning the board to face the shore, and with complete determination, exclaiming loudly to Matt, "I will stand up this time and ride it in!" I managed to stand with one leg up and one leg on one knee before the ocean swallowed me up—again! After that, we paddled into shore.

My first surfing experience lasted nearly two hours. Matt told me I was a natural.

Life is like surfing. We get knocked down again and again until we learn how to stand up more quickly and ride the waves with better balance.

FORTY-ONE

....

A LESSON FROM
THE REFINER'S FIRE

It was 2014. Wade and I had just moved into our new home in Mapleton, Utah. The house was built in 1973. We loved the idea of remodeling an older home. We saw potential. I had dreamed of having a spacious kitchen for many years. Having moved multiple time and lived on a student income for most of our marriage, I never before had been able to have my dream kitchen. This house was different. It had a strange layout with a long room running alongside the kitchen. There was this wall between them. "What if we knock down the wall? The kitchen would double in size!" we discussed it and agreed.

The home was purchased and shortly after we began the remodel. We would salvage the cabinets and have them professionally painted a beautiful cream with vintage stain. The color theme was chosen. We would have not just one but two gorgeous kitchen islands. One would be large enough to make multiple pies, roll out cinnamon roll dough, and undertake any number of projects with the kids. The other would be for serving food. Both islands would have soft-close doors and cabinets. I would have so much storage space! The thick granite slab for our countertops would be a mixture of multiple shades of white, gray, and black with specs of silver and it would offset the classic gray islands. We would have ample seating for the kids and even for entertaining as many as sixty people at once. *This will be perfect,* I thought. *I love to entertain and feed people! My large extended family will designate our home as the place to gather.*

We chose a gorgeous dark wood flooring that would offset the light cabinets. I had always loved the look of hardwood floors, especially in a kitchen. The farmhouse sink was a gorgeous too, very large and made from stainless steel. It was both practical and stylish. The faucet was tall and removable so that large soup pots could be filled beneath it. Ideal!

Weeks went by as I looked forward to being able to eat our first meal together in my dream kitchen. We were living in a mess of construction for quite some time. Dust was everywhere. Many things took longer than we had hoped. At the time, I considered it a sacrifice and stressful to be living in a mess, either eating our meals out or cooking them in the microwave in the living room. I longed for the construction just to get done. Life continued despite the massive remodel, which added to its normal chaos. At the time, I was waiting for all things to line up so that I could "get on with life."

At last, it was finished. Photos were taken and shared. Spaghetti always had been a family favorite, so this is what would be prepared for our first meal. I took a photo to commemorate the moment. The kitchen was so clean, fresh, and beautiful.

Several weeks later, I remember lying in bed dreaming of water—rushing water. It was about 3 AM. The sound continued. I stirred in my sleep as I thought of rain. Minutes went by. Then I began to wake up to the realization that the sound of water wasn't just in my dream but somewhere in the house. Climbing out of bed, I followed the sound to discover that it was coming from the kitchen.

Moving quickly and calling out to Wade, I exclaimed, "The kitchen is flooded! Come quick!" We both ran down the short flight of stairs to discover that water covered the entire brand-new wooden kitchen floor. The amount of water was not such that it could be cleaned up with a few towels. The water had poured on it. An inch of water pooled around all the newly finished cabinets too.

Frantically, we ran around the house trying to assess the damage. Our home had three levels. The bedrooms were upstairs, the main living area and kitchen were on the main floor, and there were more bedrooms and a common area in the basement. With the realization that the pouring water sounds were coming from the lowest level, we rushed downstairs. The best way to describe the scene we discovered is to say that it was raining in the basement. Not just a light rain, but a downpour!

We made a call to a restoration company. They immediately came out to begin the cleanup. All the cabinets would need to be removed, the flooring to be torn up, and the entire kitchen to be gutted and rebuilt again. We were approached by someone who worked for this company who told us he was a "contractor." He told us he could very quickly repair everything for less than what we had initially paid. He said he would work fast. Feeling both pressured and a bit desperate after so many months of previous construction, we agreed to allow him to be in charge of the remodel.

I watched as they removed the kitchen islands and began tearing up the floor. I would be once again preparing food in the microwave, which sat on a table awkwardly in the living room. I tried to see the "light" in the situation, but I really felt sorry for myself.

Soon the decision was made not only to rebuild the kitchen but also to remodel the basement. The basement ceiling had to be completely torn out, old carpet removed, and sheetrock replaced. A small kitchen and an additional bathroom would be built into the basement.

For a season, we were living in a complete mess. To walk from one room to another meant dodging large hanging sheets of plastic. Dust was everywhere. There was no escaping it. Our home and our lives were in complete chaos. The sound of industrial fans blew loudly through the house night and day to dry the floorboards. We would often leave to visit family or go to a restaurant for dinner just to escape for a few hours. I longed for it to be done so I could once again be "normal" cooking for the family, no fans, no workers in the house, and some quiet.

The lesson the refiner's fire taught me is about perspective. Looking back on these memories today, I see them as sweet, for these were the last few months we had with our son-in-law Shay. I also had no idea at the time that Wade would be leaving soon after that.

As the remodel progressed, we discovered that our contractor was not licensed and had been lining his pockets with our insurance money. He was greatly overcharging us for the work he and his crew did. Once we confronted him, he quit. We reached out to a friend who was a general contractor who finished the remodel beautifully.

The kitchen was finished in a timely manner, and it looked great. The basement was beautiful. All things were restored even better than I had hoped. But the beautiful dream I had would not be mine for long. I thought, *This home will be the home Wade and I grow old in.* But I was mistaken.

Certainly, I will always feel a connection to this house, but the memories I treasure from our time there are not those of "things." It isn't the granite countertops, the farmhouse sink, or the perfect wood floor that spring to mind when I think of it. What I treasure are the relationships that existed while I was living in the house

I have learned a valuable lesson, one that none of us should forget. *Joy is now.* If we wait until things line up perfectly to be happy, our happiness will never happen. I no longer live in that Mapleton home. What I have are just the memories.

Today Matt and I live in a home that represents our new beginning. It is my dream home not because of its size or style, but because it is filled with love. Although I sometimes contemplate remodeling the kitchen, my thoughts are different. I recognize that even if the house was to stay just as it is today, I would treasure it. Life is now. Joy can be experienced even during trials.

And with regard to raising kids, the things they will remember and treasure from home are not things at all.

FORTY-TWO

....

GRIEVE, BUT CARRY ON

Recently one of my business partners, a man based in Denmark, reached out to me. He knew Wade well. "Is it OK for me to ask you about Wade?" he asked. He was concerned that his questions would upset me.

I responded immediately, "Yes, in fact, please do. Wade is never far from my mind." Then I added, "I still cry for him even though some time has gone by."

This man and I shared online tears. He poured his heart out to me in private messages. "Wade was my spiritual brother," he told me. "I don't know how to process him being gone. It is hard to except! We were Viking brothers. It was our thing," he said. "We understood each other."

I told him, "I understand." And then I bore testimony to the healing power of the atonement and all the spiritual phenomena that had been occurring. I said, "I can smile now. I am refined. My eyes are open. Wade still exists, just in another dimension. He is actively helping each of us, the ones he loved on earth."

And I told him, "Life is eternal. We are infinite beings."

As I drove home from the gym later on the same day that this exchange had taken place, the full thrust of it hit me, and the tears flowed again. I saw and understood why. I could see how my Father in heaven has a hand in each aspect of my life. Even in pain. I saw with clarity the purpose of losing Wade as I did. My greatest fear was always the death of a loved one. I held back so much out of fear most of the time like I was emotionally holding my breath. I was afraid and lived as if, one day, when such and such thing happens, then I would be happy. And I saw that perhaps my trial had been a blessing.

Crying had become a regular part of the day. I do not want to pretend that I was fine when I was not. When any of my kids saw me weep, I would explain honestly to them that I was sad about their daddy. I didn't want to teach them to bury their feelings. I wanted them to process their emotions and cry if they needed or wanted to.

There are times when "changing the subject" so as to not have another intense cry makes sense. But in general, I wouldn't hide my tears.

Keep the routine, I would tell myself. *Choose light every moment of every day.*

FORTY-THREE

·····································

JOY IS YOUR ANSWER

Several months after returning home from Peru, I received a very special message from my sweet daughter Grace. Off the master bedroom in our home are two bathrooms, his and hers. My bathroom is quite large; it has a separate toilet area with a bidet. On the left side of the vanity is a sink above which hangs an oversized mirror with old-fashioned lights that run along its length. I frequently write messages to myself as daily reminders. Ever since the loss of Shay and Wade, Grace also has written me special little notes. They contain messages that she lovingly "feels" like she needs to write. Message such as, "Mom, you bring me joy! Dad and Shay still love you." Every message would come at the most appropriate time, during deep moments of grief and sadness. This day would be one that I would always remember. Nestled in the bottom corner of my mirror, she wrote," "Joy is your answer."

I left that little message that she had written with a bright pink chalk marker. It held even more special meaning because when I asked her why she wrote that, she replied, "I just had a feeling that I should write it."

I had no idea what was to come the following weeks. Our beloved dog, Sam, passed away suddenly. She was just a baby at three years old and truly my daughter Alyssa's best friend. While on a walk, she had consumed poison that local farmers had put out to protect the orchards surrounding our home. I had no idea that the farmers did this as we were new to this farming community. We were completely devasted. It was a very painful and traumatic death for her. The loss is still very much felt to this day. She was part of our family! I had reached a point when I angrily cried to God. "Why? After all that we have lost! Why take our precious family dog, too?" I expressed and felt anger! I had prayed fervently while Sam was under the care of the vet and unresponsive for twenty-four hours. "God, please, I know you can heal all. Please don't take our Sam." But even with my prayers, she passed away after one final seizure on Easter morning.

That morning, I faced my mirror sick with grief. There was Grace's message again: "Joy is your answer."

Our entire family was deeply grieving this loss. Many people would likely say, "This is just a dog." But if you have ever owned a dog, you know they are family. Sam was beloved. And yet she passed. Another loss. How and why? I simply didn't understand!

The sun rose and set. I was reminded again and again to surrender and trust the journey.

The losses would continue.

A short time later, I was awoken during the night to a post that Matt saw on social media. He urgently informed me that Shay's only sibling, Diana, had passed at the tender age of twenty. Diana was his younger sister. A fiery redhead, she had a beautiful singing voice and a kind heart. She had deeply loved Shay and missed him terribly. Hearing the news, I felt a whirlwind of emotions. It was as if all the old grief were opened again. I could not believe what I was hearing. *Why? How?* She had become sick with the flu and passed during the night at her parent's home.

Shay's parents had lost their only two children only a couple years apart, and both at the age of twenty! How can one family endure so much loss?

Still reeling from Diana's passing, I received another call just a few short months after Diana passing, that her father (Karl) had taken his life. The familiar sensation of shock filled my being. My heart began to race, and my stomach knotted. One of my daughters received the news while driving. She became hysterical and inconsolable. I told her to immediately find a parking lot and to stop driving. She threw herself on the ground and cried so hard at that moment that she got an untimely bloody nose. By the time I reached her, paramedics had been called by passersby. They saw a young lady screaming in the grass, covered in blood. I gathered her in my arms and firmly told her to breathe. There was a feeling of disconnect, shock, and strength that passed through my spirit and body.

There was much compassion for Shay's family. My older girls felt a kinship to Karl as he was the man who raised Shay. They had felt that they could somehow protect him and help heal his heart. They took that burden on and felt that they had failed. Hearing of his loss was too much to bear. Within the walls of my home, there were many tears shed. I could feel myself drawing up my symbolic sword to bless and protect my children. Suicide has no more place in my home! Get out of my family. Enough is enough. I fiercely reminded them of the power of God and the comfort that only He can give. Through Christ and His Atonement, healing can and will happen. Joy indeed was my answer. Remember, show your children joy. That little message she had written on my mirror became my lifeline.

I gathered them together and passionately expressed to them that it was not their job to save anyone. His passing was not their fault. I recognized that this was something that had internalized with their own father. They could not save him, either! They had carried guilt, and now it rested on Karl. It was a reflection of how they felt about their own dad. They wept and wailed. We mourned.

Then I drew my sword and said, "Enough." Each of you has a life to live. You are to take care of yourself. You set your goals, and you live life fully. This life is and will be up to each individual person on this earth. We have a path we must each walk. He knew you loved him. You could not save him. I felt the spirit flowing through me, and I understood perfectly why Grace felt prompted to write "Joy is your answer" on my mirror that day.

I fully recognized that I never could save Wade. I was not in charge of his life, either! In the end, I alone would answer to my God about my life. If it meant not listening to my intuition, I would be doing the opposite of saving my family. It wasn't about saving the family unit. This life is about me and me alone. I finally understood that just like on an airplane, I needed to put my own oxygen on first. From there, I could help others around me. But if I ignored my intuition and didn't hold healthy boundaries, all would be lost. The strength and courage I gave to my girls that dreadful day of Karl passing came through me with a force that I am only beginning to recognize. I finally understood!

Shortly after Wade passed, my dear friend, Rachelle gave me a beautiful gift. It would be one that I would treasure and would be a constant reminder that I am not alone in my pain.

"Fear not for they that be with us are more than they that be with them. Stand steadfastly in the faith of that which is to come." This was etched into a mirror in the shape of a sun. The rays were a radiant yellow-orange stained glass. The size was about the circumference of my hand outstretched. I hung this sun at the top of my kitchen window above the sink. It was a constant reminder that I would not be alone—ever.

I do believe that if we could even catch a glimpse through the veil that separates this earthly existence from the next realm, we would be both humbled and comforted knowing that there are literally legions of angels surrounding us waiting for our requests! I was indeed reminded (again) that despite our deepest heartache, we are watched over.

So many thoughts ran through my mind during those days following Karl's passing. How would I show my kids the path to joy when there was so much heartache?

I was familiar with this road.

The words came to me like a rushing wave. "You each have lives to live," I told them. "It is not your responsibility to save anyone. Each person has a choice."

The song "How Firm a Foundation" came to my mind.[3] If I put my trust in my Father in heaven, He would indeed continue to carry me. He was my foundation.

How firm a foundation, ye saints of the Lord,
Is laid for your faith in His excellent word!
What more can He say than to you He hath said,
To you who for refuge to Jesus hath fled?

In every condition, in sickness, in health,
In poverty's vale, or abounding in wealth,
At home and abroad, on the land, on the sea—

As your days may demand, so your succor shall be.

Fear not: I am with you: O, be not dismay'd!
I, I am your God, and will still give you aid;
I'll strengthen you, help you, and cause you to stand,
Upheld by my righteous, omnipotent hand.

When through the deep waters I cause you to go,
The rivers of sorrow shall not you o'erflow;
For I will be with you, your troubles to bless,
And sanctify to you your deepest distress.

When through fiery trials your pathway shall lie,
My grace, all-sufficient, shall be your supply;
The flame shall not hurt you; I only design
Your dross to consume, and your gold to refine.

E'en down to old age, all my people shall prove
My sov'reign, eternal, unchangeable love;
And when hoary hairs shall their temples adorn,
Like lambs they shall still in my bosom be borne.

The soul that on Jesus has leaned for repose
I will not, I cannot, desert to his foes;
That soul, though all hell should endeavor to shake,

Joy Is My Answer

I'll never, no never, I'll never, no never,
I'll never, no never, no never forsake!

FORTY-FOUR

....

HEALING THE EMOTIONAL BRAIN

How does one recover or heal from PTSD? I have faced this dilemma since the sudden passing of Shay. I keenly recognize that healing is a journey. At times I find myself triggered and react in such a way that I can recognize that I am indeed weak in my flesh. My spirit longs to be free, and yet I am very much having a human experience filled with all the frailties of this life.

Following Wade's death, I was shown an exercise that helps to heal the emotional brain. "Let's go back to those flashbacks," says John, my therapist. He is an individual that not only has a professional practice but also understands the trauma of survivors personally, as his own wife committed suicide years ago. He wants to know, what were the flashback scenes that I couldn't seem *not* to think about? Those moments that caused my heart to beat rapidly, my stomach to sink, and my legs to shake? He explains that this technique will take me my trauma-filled emotional brain to the next level of healing.

Even today, I still can recall those moments with such clarity that I do indeed relive them over and over on bad days, though less and less as time passes.

John and I had a chance meeting, one that affirmed my belief that there are no coincidences. When I moved my business office to a new building, he was my neighbor.

Now I am seated comfortably across from John as I begin a meditation journey. "Go back to that scene . . ." he guides me. "That scene when you got the phone call of Wade's death. What do you see? You are a witness to the scene, so to speak."

I respond, "I see myself screaming, falling to the ground, shaking. I see my family gathering around me. My sister is holding me. Brushing my hair away from my face. I hear crying. I hear screaming. I see myself shaking."

"Now," he says, "approach yourself. Tap the shoulder of yourself at that moment. Turn yourself to face the person you are today. Give an embrace to that woman who is filled with fear, anxiety, pain, shock." He paused for a moment to let me visualize it.

"Now, show yourself a vision of your future, of the woman you are today. Of where you are today. Show yourself Matt. Show her the relationship you have now. Show the laughter, the joy, the path walked. Hold that person up and tell her that it is going to be OK, and you will carry her. She doesn't need to worry. She doesn't need to be strong all the time by herself."

After a minute he continues, "And now, bring the person from that scene to sit next to you on this couch at this moment. What does she now feel? What can you tell her?" he asks.

Tears flow down my cheeks as I express that she feels warm and safe. "She knows it will all be OK," I say.

In later sessions, I began to revisit every flashback that haunted me in a similar manner, becoming like my own guardian angel. And I learned from John that this technique could be done by anyone, anywhere, and for any situation in their life that has caused them pain. It is an effective way to rewire the emotional brain.

The path to healing has many ups and downs, twists and turns, and even faceplants. As the weeks and months from the date of a loss pass, it is important for us to get help. The fact is, none of us is alone. All you have to do is ask for help. The help you receive may be from a good friend with whom you can completely let down your guard and have a good cry. It could be from a therapist trained to assist in healing from trauma. There are many peer support groups you could turn to, as well. Look for one that is specifically designed for someone with your needs.

Prayer is also one of the most powerful and underutilized resources available. Just say: "Dear Father in heaven, please help me. In Jesus' name, amen." Prayers need not be fancy. Just speak from the heart. The fact is, God already knows your heart.

After praying, we feel relief, and there is change.

FORTY-FIVE

....

JOY

For years, I lived in the "if onlys and the "shoulds," and I nearly held my breath through fleeting moments of happiness, waiting for the proverbial "other shoe" to drop. My contentment was determined by outside circumstances. I could never have imagined surviving the trials that would be mine. I lived for the future, and I lived in fear. My thoughts were: *Once Wade is done with school, and we have more money, have a bigger house, then . . .*, or, *Once the kids make better life choices, then . . .*, or, *When everyone in our family is healthy, and all things have lined up perfectly, THEN I will feel happy.* But it never happened. Once one problem was solved, another would show up. And then Wade was gone, and all that I had were the memories. The imperfect memories. The pain, the trials, the journey.

Happiness comes and goes. Joy, on the other hand, is something that can be felt even when trials persist! Joy is internal. Joy is not dependent on other people and their actions! It is a quiet peace, confidence, and understanding that everything will be OK. It is not dependent on external circumstance or even other people. It is true congruency with God, our creator. Joy comes from knowing who you are: a literal son or daughter of a loving God.

I experienced so much peace, comfort, and joy during my darkest hours following Wade's death. The greatest joy I have ever felt in my entire life has been experienced while on my knees in prayer. Joy is gratitude. Joy comes from knowing God is real, and this life is not the end!

To live joyfully means to appreciate every moment of each day.

From my experience of the refiner's fire came an understanding of joy. When my dad gave me a blessing moments after Wade's death, proclaiming that I would "have joy that I had never known" I didn't fully understand what he meant. I had hoped that my trials would be over, and my life would become smooth sailing. However, as time went on, it became clearer to me that joy is something different.

Would "the joy I have never known" mean that I would lead a life without trials and heartache? I am afraid not. I wish that I could say my trials were over! But this life is for growth. That's the human condition.

Perhaps it would mean my perspective would change? As the weeks and months after Wade's death passed, my heart did begin to change, and with that came greater understanding. I understood without a doubt that I am not alone, and that God loves me, especially because of my shortcomings, not in spite of them.

I testify that God lives and loves me. He is real. I know this. I am not living by faith alone anymore. I have felt the other side as clearly as I can feel my human frailties. I have felt, heard, and even smelled the sweetness of the spirit!

I also testify of angels! They have been there for me and continue to be each time I ask.

I will always treasure how my little girl, Grace, had the impulse to write on my mirror: "Joy is your answer." For, indeed, joy is my answer to every question and issue.

Joy is my answer for how to show up fully in my life. The greater my gratitude, the greater my joy. The more often I get down on my knees and plead for God's assistance, the more peace, and joy I feel. The more answers come.

I testify that human life is not the end! Life is eternal. Our spirits are being tested and subjected to immense growth through the experiences we call life, and we take all our lessons and insights with us when we leave our mortal bodies. What we take with us when we leave this life and transition to the next, is who we are and what we have become—even our habits and character.

I testify of a loving God.

I testify of angels that can assist in every aspect of your life!

I testify that no matter where you are in your journey, the moment you ask God will be there!

FORTY-SIX

....

THIS IS NOT THE END

Just a few short weeks after I finished writing the manuscript for this book, we had a fire that nearly caused our home to go up in smoke. The fire demolished the fourteen-by-twenty-foot shed that stood within a few feet from our home. It held all sort of yard equipment, tools, and propane tanks, as well as boxes of keepsakes. Alyssa had helped to neatly organize boxes holding important mementos, photos, journals, and personal items from years past only a week earlier. Several of these boxes held things that belonged to Wade. I had kept every pair of his shoes, including a pair of handsome cowboy boots he'd purchased just months before his passing. All his belongings were being stored with the intention of later distributing them with much thought given to our children.

Parked right alongside the shed was Wade's 1978 extended-cab highboy Ford pickup truck. He had been in the process of restoring it. He often talked about going "mudding" with our son, Wes, when he was a bit older. Many hours had been spent watching YouTube videos with our son of trucks plowing through crazy mud hills and tracks. The exterior was repainted with flat black paint, and it had a maroon interior, which was completely reupholstered.

Wade's love for old pickup trucks ran deep. His first truck was given to him at sixteen by his dad. It was radiant royal blue. He would drive that truck for many years. It was the truck in which he picked me up for our first date. He affectionally called it the Blue Dummy. Years down the road, he sold his Blue Dummy only to acquire another old fixer-upper.

The truck by the shed commanded respect from our entire family. It sat high with large tires. The hum of the engine was unmistakable. Caitlyn had expressed her plan to begin to continue to restore it only a few days prior to the fire.

So, this is what went down. I was inside puttering around one afternoon. Hearing a loud boom and crackling sounds propelled me to investigate outdoors. As I approached the back door leading to the garage, two women whom I had never met before ran into our home, screaming for keys to our cars. "Your shed is on fire! Where are your keys?" they screamed. "It is going to blow!" I lost my senses as I frantically began to search for keys to all the vehicles seconds later.

I don't recall much about what happened for the next half hour due to the urgency of the situation other than witnessing our kind neighbors with hoses working to keep the house from catching fire. Overhead, I heard the hum of a helicopter that was ready to douse the flames with a large bucket of water.

Black smoke filled the sky. The shed burned very hotly, as it was holding several sets of rubber tires. "Get the dogs in the house. Everyone, stand back!" I instructed the kids.

Matt, Wes, and his nephew had gone out target shooting. I dialed him on the phone and screamed, "Come home NOW! The shed is on fire!" He raced home.

Everything was moving so fast.

Trees set alongside the garage side of the home began to burn. The kids' playground set, complete with swings and a jungle gym, began to melt into nothing.

It was a large shed. And it became a complete inferno.

Then the firetrucks began arriving, and hoses were turned on. Kind fireman began to ask if anyone was injured. "Is everyone accounted for?" they said.

"Yes," I replied. "We are safe."

Maybe only twenty minutes had passed from that initial boom I heard.

We lost many things that day. My daughters sobbed as they witnessed their dad's pickup truck catch on fire, becoming unsalvageable. We lost journals, photos, and many things that are not replaceable.

A feeling of peace washed over me as I surveyed the charred remains of the shed and began to imagine what could have happened. I marveled at how things all "lined up." Truly, I testify of angels! Neighbors just happened to be driving by and saw the fire. These kind women ran into my home to find me! No one was hurt! But still, my heart did ache that day for the loss of those irreplaceable mementos.

The cause of the fire was accidental. Matt had been spraying weeds with a fire torch just outside the shed. He very carefully set the torch away from where little hands could touch it when he was finished. It was turned off and propped so as not to touch anything flammable in the shed or fall, for that matter! But while he was out shooting with the boys, it had somehow fallen anyhow. It still makes no sense how this could have happened.

In subsequent days, I received several messages from people in different areas of my life. They all proclaimed the same message: "Wade wants you to move forward." "Do not keep his things anymore." "Release the past pain." "He isn't attached any longer to his stuff." "Move forward!" "Do not cling to his things any longer!"

Also came the beautiful message: "He is very much watching over you all, and you were all protected and in no danger."

As the family began to carefully sift through the burned items in the remnants of the shed, Brianna came across a few items that were preserved. She unearthed several family photos as well as a letter Wade had written to her just weeks before his passing. Very gently, she placed those precious items in a clear plastic bag. The letter read: "I love you, love Dad."

EPILOGUE

I started writing my experiences down after Shay and Wade's deaths because I realized that others may want to know of the comfort available to them from heaven.

It's been nearly three years since Wade's passing, and life seems to continue faster as I get older. There seems to always be a challenge of some sort. However, I have been forever changed by the experiences and feelings that I was able to receive through my prayers and supplication to God. These feelings and experiences give me a new perspective on my life. Material things don't matter that much to me. I have a comfort and peace that is always with me. I know that there is a purpose to this life. I know that there is life beyond this one.

Through these past several years, I have been able to understand the role of Jesus Christ in our lives. I have felt His understanding and love for us. My sense of purpose is to focus on loving my family, and those around me.

I may never fully understand mental illness or how to best help those with this struggle, but I do know that the spouses of loved ones with this illness need not suffer throughout this life. It's important to set boundaries and stand by them. Life is too short to be held hostage by someone's instability.

Be courageous in your efforts to live authentically and pursue your dreams and the life you know is available to you. Throughout the inevitable struggles you will face in this noble pursuit, please know there is loving support and heavenly help waiting to answer your prayers.

NOTES

1. Jeffrey R. Holland. "The Ministry of Angels," *Ensign,* vol. 38, no. 11 (November 2008), p. 29.

2. Reinhold Niebuhr. "The Serenity Prayer" was written for a sermon given at Heath Evangelic Union Church in Heath, Massachusetts, in 1934, and subsequently was used by Niebuhr on many other occasions. Its first publication was in 1951 in a newspaper column.

3. Source: https://hymnary.org/text/i_know_that_my_redeemer_lives_what_joy#Author. Samuel Medley (1738–1799) was a Baptist minister who preached in Liverpool, England, in the second half of the eighteenth century and wrote many popular hymns. For more details on his biography and music, see: https://hymnary.org/person/Medley_S.

4. Originally published in Rippon's *A Selection of Hymns* (1787), where the lyricist is identified only as K. It has been variously attributed to George Keith (1787) or Robert Keen (c. 1787). For more details, see: https://hymnary.org/text/how_firm_a_foundation_y e_saints_of.

RESOURCES

Here are a few resources you may find helpful if you or your loved ones are going through the refiner's fire. To begin, please visit my website, www.LauraStoker.com, and join me on the social networks.

- Instagram: LauraStoker13
- Facebook: Author Laura Stoker

HEALING HANDS FOUNDATION

The dōTERRA Healing Hands Foundation is working to give voice to those who have been silenced by poverty, trafficking, and other unpropitious circumstances. Visit the website: https://doterrahealinghands.org

SUICIDE PREVENTION LIFELINE

If you or someone you love is feeling depressed or having thoughts of suicide, please call the National Suicide Prevention Lifeline 1-800-273-8255.

The Lifeline provides 24/7, free and confidential support for people in distress, prevention and crisis resources for you or your loved ones, and best practices for professionals. Deaf and hard of hearing people may chat with Lifeline online at the website:

SuicidePreventionLifeline.org

FOR COPING WITH TRAUMA

Emotional Superpowers
www.emotionalsuperpowers.com

WOMEN'S BETRAYAL TRAUMA GROUP

S.A. Lifeline Foundation/SAL 12Step
www.salifeline.org

ABOUT THE AUTHOR

Laura Stoker is an entrepreneur. She is passionate about empowering others, most particularly women, to achieve financial independence. She teaches them how to make high six-figure incomes while having the time freedom to be with their babies at home. She is a leader in dōTERRA, with a team of over 150,000 that spans the globe.

Laura enjoys hiking, running, and being active. She is a certified yoga teacher and stars in her own DVD

Essential Yoga. She has been featured on her local TV station in Utah, sharing her yoga and some of her favorite healthy recipes. She also loves spending time with her husband, Matt, and their blended family of nine kids and one sweet grandson. On their property in Payson, Utah, they care for chickens, ducks, bunnies, cats, and dogs. Laura is a hobby breeder of Bernedoodles.